Nourished

Also by Becky Johnson and Rachel Randolph

We Laugh, We Cry, We Cook

*A Mom and Daughter Dish
about the Food That Delights Them
and the Love That Binds Them*

Nourished

A SEARCH *for* HEALTH, HAPPINESS, *and a* FULL NIGHT'S SLEEP

Becky Johnson
and Rachel Randolph

ZONDERVAN

Nourished
Copyright © 2014 by Becky Johnson and Rachel Randolph

This title is also available as a Zondervan ebook. Visit www.zondervan.com/ebooks.

Requests for information should be addressed to:

Zondervan, 3900 *Sparks Dr. SE, Grand Rapids, Michigan 49546*

Library of Congress Cataloging-in-Publication Data

Johnson, Becky Freeman, 1959-
　　　Nourished : a search for health, happiness, and a full night's sleep / Becky
　　Johnson and Rachel Randolph.
　　　　　pages cm
　　　ISBN 978-0-310-33101-8 (softcover)
　　　　1. Christian women--Religious life. 2. Well-being--Religious aspects--
　　Christianity. 3. Randolph, Rachel, 1983- I. Title.
　　BV4527.J6335 2015
　　248.8'43--dc23　　　　　　　　　　　　　　　　　　　　　　　　　2014026270

Published in association with the literary agency of WordServe Literary Group, Ltd.,
Highlands Ranch, Colorado 80130 (www.wordserveliterary.com).

Cover design: Connie Gabbert
Cover and interior photography: © Maglara / Shutterstock®
Interior design: Beth Shagene

First Printing November 2014 / Printed in the United States of America

To Ruthie
Beloved Mother and "Granny"

Whose life has been a blessed
and nourishing role model for all

~

Contents

Invitation to a More Nourishing Life

*Nourishing yourself in a way that helps you blossom
in the direction you want to go is attainable,
and you are worth the effort.*
Deborah Day

One thing we, as mom and daughter, have learned the hard way: women cannot afford to put off self-care until "life eases up," "the toddlers are in school," "the kids leave for college," or "we're through with the crisis at hand." It was precisely in the moments of complete overwhelm that we realized if we did not start practicing nourishing routines, we would sink. And if Mama starts going down, the whole family ship goes on tilt with her. Whether you are twenty or fifty, burning the career candle at both ends, or cleaning up baby messes at both ends, it's vital to know how to put emotional oxygen over your own mouth regularly, before some ER nurse does it for you, literally (though we've both been exhausted enough for a little nap on a hospital gurney to sound rather lovely).

The tone we want to set in this book is not one of a therapist, life coach, personal trainer, or self-help guru—though we've collectively watched enough talk shows, done enough lay counseling and mentoring, and led enough food discussions and exercise classes to push a few motivational buttons when needed. Plus we've long been practicing our own form of kitchen-table therapy, without a license, on our family and friends until they either start to feel better or get tired of humoring us.

Mostly, we are empathic friends in the process of learning to better nourish our own lives and hope you can profit from reading about our journeys. Or at least be entertained by them. We will share not only our successes but our failures, because as women who love to laugh, we find it is usually the miserable flops that make the most hilarious stories. In addition, failures have a way of teaching their own searing brand of lessons we never forget.

In her book *When the Heart Waits*, Sue Monk Kidd wrote, "Crisis is an invitation to cross a threshold." Whether your crisis is a true-life drama, an existential crisis where you are searching for more joy and meaning, or a mini-crisis, like a bad day where you just need us to say, "Take a guilt-free nap!" or "Put your feet up and enjoy a latte!"—we invite you to join us in crossing new thresholds to more nourishing ways of living, moving, and being.

> The LORD will guide you continually,
> And satisfy your soul in drought,
> And strengthen your bones;
> You shall be like a watered garden,
> And like a spring of water, whose waters do not fail.
> Isaiah 58:11 NKJV

A NOTE FROM BECKY (THE MOM) AND RACHEL (THE DAUGHTER)

We will take turns "talking" in the book, like Kathie Lee and Hoda, only on paper and with less interrupting. We'll indicate who is talking by putting our names before our individual sections.

We know.

Brilliant.

— PART 1 —

Nourished 911

Chapter 1

Meltdown on Aisle Three

Signs of an "Under-Nourished" Woman

Seeds of faith are always within us;
sometimes it takes a crisis to nourish
and encourage their growth.
Susan Taylor

BECKY

It's not a major crisis that will typically cause a woman to melt down. Forces somehow rally to meet these big challenges when they come. It's the little things, the drip-drip-drip of Chinese torture, the dozens of daily irritations that, over time, can send us straight into the fetal position crying for our mommy. Or God. Or chocolate. Or medication. Or all four, depending on the day.

Most of us have experienced wake-up moments when we realize that life, as we are doing it, isn't working.

I experienced just such a wake-up call about a year and a half ago, with the imminent arrival of the Thanksgiving holiday. This particular year I planned to hostess, entertain, and cook for eight live-in family guests for eight straight days and nights. (We call it

Thanksgiving Camp. Most of my friends call it Becky's Insanity.)
Three months earlier, Greg and I agreed to let our twenty-five-
year-old nephew come stay with us until he found a job in Colorado, where we live and where he wanted to start fresh. He arrived
in late August, but unfortunately, by the third week in November,
no job had yet materialized. Greg and I had been empty nesters
for a decade, and as much as we love our nephew, we were missing
the freedom of our former "Just You 'n' Me" lives. On top of these
adjustments, we were anticipating a horde of guests on their way
for a week of nonstop fun and turkey. Our five-year-old grandson,
Georgie, who lived in Seattle, would also be joining us, sans parents, via his first solo flight. (I should mention here that everyone
else calls Georgie by his given name, George—my father's name.
But he told me that I could call him "Georgie" forever if I want to
because "you are my Nonny." And, so, I want to.)

Normally, I get a charge out of playing Holiday Camp Director, but my reserves had been depleted by other stressors, and
somewhere on aisle 13 at our local King Soopers Grocery store, I
started to tremble. I looked at my long list of To Dos and To Buys,
and suddenly none of it made sense. I could feel my heart racing,
perspiration beading on my forehead. Still shaking, I steered my
cart over to the mini-clinic attached to the back of the store. My
pulse was sky high. The physician's assistant there immediately
directed me to the "real" doctor's office across the street, a more
medical-looking facility that did not also house a bakery depart-
ment and produce aisle.

The doctor gave me a prescription to slow my heart rate, but
what she did that helped most was to tell me: "Sweetie, if you don't
slow down, the only thing plucked, roasted, and lying face-up on
your Thanksgiving table is going to be you." She asked to look
at the list I'd been mumbling about and said, "You need to cross
out about a third of these things; they probably don't need to be
done at all. At least not today. Then delegate another third." She

handed the list back. "That should not only help your heart rate and keep you alive through the holidays, but it might even allow you to have some fun."

By the time I got home with my prescription filled and my newly edited list, I was already calming down. I looked at the kitchen clock. There were planes full of people en route, winging their way to the Denver airport. No time for a nap, but I delegated what I could to my husband Greg, then dove into the kitchen to bake pies and cakes for the approaching army. I alternated sips of coffee (for energy) with deep breathing (to relax). In other words, I did the best I could with what I had to work with at the time.

The first person scheduled to arrive would be Georgie. On my way to Denver International, thoughts of seeing this dark-eyed, good-natured, beloved grandboy absorbed all my focus; any concerns beyond getting him safely into my arms fell away like a heavy coat, dropping to the floor with a careless thud.

Once at the gate, my heart leapt at the sight of Georgie coming off the plane, his smiling face snuggled in the hood of his winter coat as he held his beloved Pillow Pet in both hands, his backpack bouncing behind him. He ran into my arms, joyfully shouting "Noooooonnnnyyy!!!" as I bent down to smother him with grandma love. The flight attendant holding his hand looked at me and grinned. "He did great! It's pretty obvious he knows you, but I still have to see some ID."

Once the formalities were over, I took Georgie's hand and asked, "What was the best part of the airplane ride?"

"Being brave!" he replied proudly.

I smiled at his shining eyes, all remnants of anxiety fading fast, replaced by the high of being in full-throttle grandma mode. How is it that children are so adept at bringing what matters most into sudden, sharp focus? If a five-year-old could courageously and good-naturedly fly three hours on a plane alone to see his Nonny and Poppy, surely I could tackle Thanksgiving week without flying over the cuckoo's nest. My focus shifted from "so much I have to do" to "the family I want to enjoy and love."

When my daughter Rachel, her husband Jared, and their baby, Jackson, arrived from Texas by plane the next day, her presence further lifted and soothed my mood. I was impressed by Rachel's maturity and serenity that week. She had a sense of calm that was contagious. Thanksgiving Camp went off without a hitch, and we made lots of happy memories. As soon as the last bit of company flew away, I fell into bed and slept like a baby for almost twenty-four hours. And I would need that rest. Because soon our lives would rise to a whole new level of crazy.

RACHEL

My tipping point, though less dramatic than Mom's, came the first time I left my son overnight so I could go on a girl's weekend. At the hotel I began to realize I'd dropped so many small and pleasurable routines that once kept me sane and balanced: taking a hot shower alone in complete silence, carefully stroking mascara onto my lashes and curling them up just so, going to a café to enjoy a latte and a book while people strolled by. Over the first year of motherhood, I'd focused so completely on Jackson's well-being I had all but lost *me*.

As it turned out, I ran into an old friend on that getaway. She was creative and energetic. Her hair was washed and styled daily. Getting dressed, for her, meant more than putting on a bra under the tank top she'd just slept in and slipping on the first pair of athletic shorts she found on her closet floor. She ate well, she slept well, and she even woke up early with a spring in her step — precoffee. I noticed how she sensed God's presence and heard his whispers of love to her heart. She spent time sitting, praying, and pondering.

I missed this old friend. I cried tears of joy for our sweet reunion. And I enthusiastically invited her to come home with me, to meet my son, and to reconnect with my husband. I'd found my old self, and I didn't want to say goodbye ... again.

But how would I fit *this woman* into *that woman's* life? The life where I was raising a soon-to-be toddler and writing a book, at the start of my coaching husband's busy football season.

When I returned home I made one small step toward getting reacquainted with the old me. I scheduled Jackson for two days of Mother's Day Out per week. It is a wonderful program, highly recommended by friends I trusted. Finally, regular time all to myself ... to dream, think, and write.

Or so I thought.

I loved the free time, but finding the right "space" to write near Jackson's Mother's Day Out proved tricky. I tried "The Great American Community Office," Starbucks, but finding a vacant chair near an outlet for my laptop was always a challenge. On top of this, Texans are born chatterers, raised to believe that "shooting the breeze" with strangers is part of being socially gracious. So even with my laptop up and my headphones on, some friendly soul would inevitably pull up a chair to chat and ask, "Whatcha workin' on?"

The answer to this second dilemma came when our friend Nick started a coworking space called Common Desk in Deep Ellum, an artsy part of downtown Dallas. I took the "self-care" plunge and, using some of my advance money, signed up for a membership. Having a fun place to "go to work" while Jackson was at Mother's Day Out gave me a good reason to wash my hair and get dressed up in clothes that weren't scrounged from my closet floor. Now, with both time and space in place, my writing days became a joy.

On my first day "at the office," I sat down next to a young woman in her late twenties. She looked so put together in her pencil skirt and button-up blouse. Her straight-cut blond hair framed a friendly face. She looked up at me, gray-blue eyes sparkling, and smiled broadly. "Hi, I'm Megan."

I opened up my diaper bag and pulled my laptop out of the changing pad compartment. "Hi, I'm Rachel."

"I see you're a mom too," she said, pointing to her own double-duty bag sitting beside her.

"Yep, a one-year-old boy. And you?"

"A two-year-old daughter."

Over snippets of small talk, I discovered Megan was a budding architect and we both happened to live in the same small town. She shared that climbing the corporate ladder didn't fit with her desire to be a hands-on mom. Taking a sip of coffee, she explained, "I want to be home nights and weekends. I want a life outside the office with my family." So Megan quit her high-paying corporate job to start her own architecture business from scratch. Instead of fitting her life into the "stay-at-home mom box" or "the corporate woman box," she designed a life that embraced both passions. I liked her immediately.

"Want to run out for a quick lunch?" Megan asked one day. She knew I was vegan and said she had a great spot in mind.

"It's not in the best part of town," she warned as we pulled into a gravel parking lot behind a run-down building, "but it's the best around. Everyone who knows good Thai, knows to come here." And so I had my first Thai food experience, falling in love with basil noodles — a dish of thick flat rice noodles and bright vegetables stirred into a sweet sticky sauce with fresh basil and a kick of heat.

How long had it been since I'd grabbed lunch with a girlfriend (not counting picnic lunches at the playground)? Megan and I talked about the projects we were working on, about the cute (and irritating) things our toddlers were doing these days. She gave me some logistical tips for getting out of the house on time with bags packed, lunches made, and no crucial binkies or blankies left behind, so I could take advantage of all five hours of my time away.

The sun shone on us as we carefully walked over the gravel in our strappy dress sandals back to the car. Sounds of children laughing in a schoolyard filled the air. I thought of Jackson playing at school with his classmates, laughing and developing his own friendships. My soul was nourished, and I sensed his was being nourished as well.

A few weeks later, on a crisp November day, while sitting in a comfy retro red swivel chair at Common Desk, I typed the last words of my first book. As soon as Megan walked in the door, I spun around in my chair. Trying not to distract everyone else in the room, I whisper-squealed, "I finished it!" Megan had just come from a meeting with a potential new client and had good news of her own: she'd won a bid on a big contract and secured the project. We were giddy with excitement, two young moms putting a lot on the line to follow our dreams ... and today, life seemed to be going our way.

By the time of our Thanksgiving trip to Colorado, it was evident in my relaxed demeanor that I'd made some significant changes. Mom commented on how at ease I seemed to be in handling the challenges that come with traveling with an almost eighteen-month-old. I was actually surprised as well, remembering the previous trips I'd made to Colorado with Jackson and how frazzled I'd felt.

I could hardly believe how one nourishing act of self-care had made so much difference. I felt more balanced, more present for my career, my family, and myself. Seeing that simple changes could return big results, I was newly motivated to address other areas of my life still dragging me down. I wondered, Hmm ... could I connect with the runner I used to be in my energetic early twenties? The organized, financially savvy me? The me who made regular time for meaningful friendships? Where might I take me that I'd never been before? Maybe there's a version of me I've not even met yet. A me who isn't afraid and anxious, who makes quick, confident decisions without her perfectionist doubts looming over her. The possibilities for a new, improved me felt endless and exciting.

I knew I couldn't tackle everything at once, but I could focus on one area of my life at a time, make one change, and see where it might lead me at the end of, say, a year.

Bill O'Hanlon, one of the pioneers of solution-oriented therapy (sometimes called "brief therapy"), wrote, "Whenever you are stuck with a problem, try something new. Do something—just one thing—different. Break the pattern of the problem."[1] I liked the sound of that. At the very least it was someplace to start.

Chapter 2

Jumping Off Tall Buildings

Nourish or Perish

*Don't forget to pause and nourish yourself
a bit along the way. When you're born to help others
sometimes you forget to help yourself.*
Paula Heller Garland

BECKY

No sooner had I cleared out Thanksgiving Camp than I received a phone call that would upend everything again. On the other end of the line was Georgie's mother. She wondered about the possibility of Georgie and her moving in with us for a while to test out the job market in Denver. I, of course, jumped for joy at the chance. We'd get to enjoy the rare gift of spending lots of time with our grandson and help our daughter-in-law, who was a single mom, with Georgie's care. (Legally, she was our ex-daughter-in-law, since she and Zach had divorced a year before, but she had become a part of our family, and their divorce had not changed those feelings. Georgie's dad, my eldest son, was a commercial fisherman, gone many months at a time.)

And yet, I was taxed to the max by the tower of plates I was already spinning. As much as my heart squealed, "Yes!"—what resources would I draw upon to rise to more, when I was already running on less?

John Eldredge wrote, "Being in partnership with God ... often feels ... like being Mel Gibson's sidekick in the movie *Lethal Weapon*. In his determination to deal with the bad guy, he leaps from seventh-story balconies into swimming pools, surprised that we would have any hesitation in following after him."[2] In my forty years of being a Christ follower, no picture of God has ever resonated more with me. Being God's friend—especially when He asks us to put down our prepared script and jump into His live-action movie—is both terrifying and exhilarating.

It didn't take long for Greg and me to choose to jump off the seven-story building; we enthusiastically agreed to welcome our grandson and his mom into our home for as long as they needed to live there to get on their feet and out on their own.

So this is how it came to be that Greg and I expanded our former role as empty-nesting honeymooners to become patriarch and matriarch of a unique patched-together family of five.

How would I survive more changes, more people in the house, caring for my grandson part time, plus regularly cooking big family meals for the whole *Hee Haw* gang?

It didn't take long before I came to the divine realization that if I were going to survive a life of more pouring out, physically and emotionally, I must be more diligent about pauses for refilling. I needed to regularly nourish myself if I was going to take on caring for so many others.

RACHEL

God hasn't asked me to jump off a tall building lately. However, I did go grocery shopping with a two-year-old the other day. That kind of made me want to jump off a tall building. Does that count?

For the moment, I'm just leaping from stone to stone in a mostly gentle river. Though some days it takes every bit of energy and sanity I have to make those leaps. Being a mother to a toddler takes a constant flow of energy and courage as I jump from river rock to river rock. Mom's life requires great bursts of energy for relatively short periods of time, but as she reminds me, in between those high-energy times of caring for a lot of people at once, she and Greg get lots of long breaks—George goes to school, they both take naps, and they frequently travel away together for weekend or weeklong breaks.

I wonder about you, out there, reading this book today. What kind of nourishment do you need most for the pace and challenges of your unique life? David, the wild-hearted Shepherd-Warrior-King, wrote psalms full of prayers for superhuman energy bursts.

> *For by You I can run against a troop,*
> *By my God I can leap over a wall.*
> Psalm 18:29 NKJV

We all need bursts of that Davidic energy at times, like Red Bull for the soul. But mostly I need steady nourishment in the nonstop caring for a little one, especially during football and baseball season when my husband's coaching job keeps him gone late hours. Most days my prayers are less like David's and more like Paul's encouragement to the Galatians: "And let us not grow weary of doing good, for in due season we will reap, if we do not give up" (Galatians 6:9 ESV).

What I need are regular sips of green smoothies for the soul.

～

Recently mom emailed me a study showing that men typically get stressed about just one thing, mostly their jobs. The cure is equally simple: the TV remote. (Color us "not shocked.") Women, on the other hand, tend to get stressed about a whole universe of issues and recover in a much wider variety of ways.

Mom and I did a little informal survey of the "daily stuff" that stressed out our women friends. Putting the issues in related piles, we came up with the following catchall list of everyday stuff that bogs us down, holds us back, and steps on our last frayed nerve.

TOP TEN EVERYDAY STRESSORS OF WOMEN

1. **Stress of Chaotic Surroundings:** The nonstop influx of clutter, drudgery of housekeeping, and general feeling of being overwhelmed and disorganized; or living in surroundings that don't really reflect our personalities or inspire us.

2. **Stress of Schedules:** Too much to do, too many needs to meet, difficulty accepting limitations, inability to say no or ask for help without guilt. Not enough time for solitude, treating yourself, being creative. The difficulties of finding work you love and then balancing it with the rest of your life, or family. Not to mention, the challenge of doing all this within a budget.

3. **Stress of Negative Body Image:** The inability to love our bodies as they really are or to cope with "mom bodies" after babies and the angst of aging. In other words, the stress of not being Angelina Jolie.

4. **Stress of Negative Self-Talk:** Thought patterns that wear us out, make us anxious, or send us into a downward spiral of unending despair and crankiness.

5. **Stress of Food Issues:** From trying to eat healthy while craving a Big Mac, to the chore of feeding a hungry family — Every. Single. Day.

6. **Stress of Fitness:** Guilt about not exercising enough, guilt about the time it takes to get fit (time away from loved ones or

---

responsibilities), getting discouraged with slow results. In short, not being able to run a mile and instantly, permanently, lose twenty pounds without ever having to repeat the ordeal again.

7. **Stress of Friendship:** How to find friends you really like and admire who also think you are equally endearing. How to handle toxic or draining relationships without getting kidnapped by negativity.

8. **Stress of Marriage:** Making time for each other and finding ways to replenish our love tanks. How to stay in touch with our sensuous side — even if we are covered in baby spit-up and peanut-butter handprints.

9. **Stress of Raising Children:** Whether your child is two or twenty-five, being a parent can keep you scurrying and worrying. We want to enjoy our kids — really we do. And most of us feel we could do that. Definitely. If we only had to parent our children when we were well rested and feeling up to it. All we need is a bevy of downstairs servants at our beck and call to nanny our children, cook our meals, dress and undress us in the latest fashions, tuck us in bed at night, and serve us a lovely homemade breakfast on a tray. (I just realized that this job description could fit either "The entire serving staff of *Downton Abbey*," or "What Every Mom Does for Their Kids Every Day." No wonder we're tired.)

10. **Stress of Feeling like a Spiritual Slacker:** Struggling with a nagging vague feeling that we're never doing enough for God, not paying him the right kind of attention, or practicing spiritual disciplines with enough ... uh ... discipline. In other words, we struggle with the feeling that God is like our first-grade piano teacher who knows we haven't practiced "Hot Cross Buns" even once all week, though we're doing our best to dance and slide our fingers across the keyboard in ways that look really impressive.

Reading over this list, Mom and I felt two emotions at once: recognition and hope. Recognition as we both raise our hands in empathy with each of the common stressors above. And hope because we know one of the greatest ways to make a real change or learn a new way of being is to research, experiment, write about it, and then *do* it!

After looking at this list, we figured we could either bond into the deep end of insanity together as our lives spiraled out of control, or we could find a way to make our lives work for us and our families in ways that were more nourishing. To get from here to there, we looked at the list above and reframed the stressors in more positive ways. The result formed the outline of this book, which also became our list of goals for our own lives in the coming months.

As coauthors of a previous book that shares our mutual love for food and cooking, we resonated with the word *nourish* as a metaphor for living in more delectable, healthy, and life-giving ways. We wanted to give women permission to pause and ask themselves, "How can I better nourish my life? What would it look like to feel nourished at the end of each day? To be well fed in body, mind, emotions, and soul, no matter how impossibly busy or stressed out our outer worlds may be?"

BECKY

Rachel is obviously in the "young marriage, new mom" stage of life, but not far removed from her earlier career-woman days, so she brings her unique twenty-something-going-on-thirty-something struggles to this book. I am in the "midlife, grandparenting, hot-flashing" stage of life with my own set of "special issues." We found ourselves both longing for a full night's sleep these past couple of years, but for different reasons: Rachel's teething baby was keeping her up at night; my hormones were waking me in the wee hours. Rachel has precious little time to dash on makeup and do her hair because she has a two-year-old hugging her legs. I have more free time to do my makeup, and no toddler is currently attached to my shin, but the job of spackling and grouting middle-aged wrinkles calls for at least an extra ten minutes per day.

We recently talked about how it often doesn't take much to end our days feeling more nourished and less drained. A few tweaks can go a long way in improving the quality of a busy woman's life. A little time out for a good morning conversation with God before getting out of bed. An impromptu walk in the sunshine. A lunch out with an empathic friend. A romantic embrace from our loving husbands. A guilt-free nap. A perfect latte enjoyed in twenty minutes of complete solitude. All these small gifts to ourselves add up, like deposits to our Mood and Energy Account, to give us more nourishing days that lead eventually to better-nourished lives.

We were eager students, ready to go down the list of stressors and find more peaceful ways of dealing with them, one at a time.

But before we dived in, I was curious about one thing: "How do we make sure that any changes we implement last more than a couple of weeks? What, in fact, motivates us to change and then turns those changes into nourishing habits?"

I would find to my surprise that it would have something to do with listening to elephants.

Chapter 3

Sticky Changes

Nourishing Habits That Stay

If you don't like something, change it;
if you can't change it,
change the way you think about it.
Mary Engelbreit

RACHEL

When Jackson was a little less than a year old, and my first book deadline was looming, I realized my life, such as it was, was not working. I never seemed to meet all the expectations others had for me or that I had set for myself. No matter how hard I tried to prioritize my days, something or someone was forever being left out. And no matter how carefully I planned, there just wasn't time for all I needed (or wanted) to do.

The result? Guilt. Constant guilt.

A planner by nature, I decided to orchestrate an instant, all-encompassing makeover of my life. So on a Sunday afternoon, I opened up Excel on my computer and made spreadsheets and chore charts and printed off a calendar for the week with every day's agenda. The plans and goals included (but were not limited to) making time for prayer, planning and cooking healthy meals, exercising daily, getting the house cleaned and organized and keeping it that way, spending time with my husband and baby, and pursuing my writing.

I posted all of the lists right on the refrigerator door so I could be reminded of my goals all day long at a glance. It felt so good to stand back and look at my charts. Ambition taking over good sense, I added the following to the list: "Cut back on caffeine: Skip morning coffee and take a brisk morning walk every day instead." Now that I'd planned my work, I couldn't wait for morning to come, and start "workin' my plan." I was floating on a high of imagining my new, improved, healthy, happy, organized life.

After church Sunday evening, I got the first hint that things might not go quite as well as I hoped.

Jackson seemed fussy, so I grabbed the thermometer. Sure enough he had a fever. I was up most of the night trying to help him get comfortable, praying for sleep that didn't come. By Monday morning, just when I thought I might have him settled down enough to sleep, the doorbell rang. At 7:30 a.m. nobody who knows me (and likes me) would ring the doorbell that early. The loud chime throughout the house had me and my baby wide awake again. *We might as well get up and see who would dare to wake a young mom and her baby*, I thought.

Hurrying out of my pj's and into a T-shirt and sweats, throwing my wild morning curls into a bun, I wearily wandered to the front door with Jackson on my hip, still in his footie pajamas. On the way there, I cast a longing glance at the coffeemaker, my anti-caffeine resolve already weakening in my sleep-deprived state.

Standing at the door was a girl in her young twenties who looked as though her morning routine might have resembled mine, except she'd thrown on some wrinkled black scrubs instead of sweats. At first I thought she might have intentionally gelled her tresses into one of those "cool, messy hair" hipster dos. But upon closer examination, no. It appeared she'd woken up (probably running late) and decided to skip the hassle of a hairbrush altogether.

She pushed away some stiff strands of bed head. "I'm here to give you your physical for the life insurance policy."

"Hi, yes, well," I stammered, "my husband mentioned this would happen, but we called the insurance company and rescheduled the appointment for next week, later in the day. When I might actually be awake and aware."

This girl didn't get the memo. She just stood there like a lost puppy, mumbling. "They told me to come here, though. I, uh, I don't know where else to go." Her eyes were big, round, tired, and possibly hungover. I couldn't just close the door and turn her away.

Shrugging my shoulders and waving her in, I apologized for the messy house and headed straight for the coffeemaker, offering to make her a cup. I made it strong, with enough for a large mug for me too, as it was clear we were both going to need more than a brisk walk to make it through this day. I'd decaffeinate tomorrow.

The young woman sat down at my kitchen table and pulled out a survey from her bag as I bounced Jackson on my knee. In a mumbled monotone, eyes darting everywhere but in my direction, she asked no less than a hundred questions regarding the diseases I may or may not have contracted (and the activities I may or may not have participated in to contract said diseases).

After the parade of questions, she handed me a small cup and asked me to give her a urine sample. Thankfully, she did let me excuse myself to perform this function in the restroom. Otherwise, the awkwardness level would have risen off the charts. Getting the liquid gold into the cup proved to be no easy task while holding a clingy sick baby who cried every time I set him down, but we managed. Then came the fun part—the blood draw. She looked more frightened by the needles than I did. It took her two shaky attempts, and she left my arm black-and-blue and sore for almost a week.

The visit couldn't have been less pleasant or less awkward. Apparently, you don't need any social skills or experience with needles (or a comb) to be an in-home nurse for this particular company.

I know, I know. "Life is what happens when you make other plans." Yeah, well, Life and I were not on great speaking terms that day. I sat and sipped my coffee in a cloud of defeated gloom as I watched my productive "makeover" chart sail out an imaginary window.

I looked at what I'd written on my to-do list for the day. "Plan a week's worth of menus and shop for groceries." I looked at the feverish baby in my immobile arm and wearily scratched that off with my free hand. My own spike in temperature followed later that afternoon, and whatever might have been left of my waning ambition fizzled into nothing but a desire to sleep for a hundred years.

Within a week Jackson and I were both well, but I'd fallen even further behind. The spreadsheets and charts I'd made in a frenzy of excitement now overwhelmed me. And the thought of life without coffee in it made me want to curl up and die.

I was right back where I'd started: overwhelmed, full of guilt, and unsure how to make my life work.

What had gone so wrong so fast? Was it just circumstances out of my control? Was I lacking willpower? Had I set myself up for failure by tackling too much?

BECKY

Why Change Is So Hard

When you look at all the areas of your life that may need to change for you to live more nourished and less stressed, even this can feel overwhelming. Where to begin? How to begin? And how many times have we enthusiastically announced we're ready to make a *big change!* — only to fall back into comfortable but unsatisfying routines?

Like Rachel, I'd made several similar attempts in my past to revamp my life, only to find myself right back where I'd started: still searching for my keys every time I left the house; still unable to create and stick with a system; still in the jeans I'd once dubbed my "bloat jeans," which morphed into my "everyday jeans"; still giving to others while neglecting self-care.

A good friend who is also a therapist once told me that people who come to see him are often stuck in a state he called "stable misery"—a place people tend to park and stall out on their own lives. Most people don't make radical adjustments for the better because the discomfort and uncertainty of change is more frightening than the current misery they've grown comfortable with.

That was an ah-ha moment for me. Yes, most often, people change for good (including myself) when life gives them a wake-up call or the discomfort grows to a point where the misery finally outweighs the fear of making a change. As someone once said, "The day came when the risk to remain tight in a bud was more painful than the risk it took to blossom."[3] How true is that? Most of us wait until things get really miserable before we're determined enough to change our habits.

Even though most people don't change until a crisis hits or the misery mounts to unbearable levels, the good news is that you and I do not have to be "most people." We can make a choice to change without going through a crisis or meltdown. We really can proactively choose to live a more nourishing life and make small adjustments that yield happier dividends, without years of misery or sudden crisis. In truth, the wisest, happiest women pause to consider their life on a regular basis. They interrupt the nonstop flow of activity now and again to ask, "What can I tweak in my life to experience less stress and more joy?" They don't see life as dictated by fate; they see it as a series of choices and actions. They see options and open windows with new vistas, where others see slammed, locked doors.

There are several paths to making more positive, nourishing changes. In fact, entire books and research studies are devoted to the subject of how people change or don't change. The subject has fascinated me for years, and I can't seem to get enough of it. Some paths are radical, exhausting, and painful but promise more immediate results. (Think *Extreme Home Makeover* or *Biggest Loser*.) Other researchers posit that lasting change happens best one teeny-tiny change at a time, drawn out over a long period. Both paths have worked for different people in different circumstances.

Certainly, personality types weigh into preferences for making a change, but life circumstances also play a part. My energetic daughter is, by nature, more of an extreme get-'er-done gal; I'm more of a "porch swing and hammock" girl. I prefer slower, gentler paths to change. Even so, outside circumstances have at times forced sudden and radical changes in my life, leaving my head spinning. But once the spinning stops, I'm often amazed at the good changes left in the wake of an unexpected challenge. Now that Rachel is a mother, she's experiencing limits to her preference for radical shifts. She may long for an extreme program, to jump on the fast track to major change. But her life is now dictated by a toddler's pace, which doesn't allow her the luxury of get-'er-done projects. Like all moms of kids at home, her life is no longer completely her own; she'll have to work around a young child's needs to accomplish new goals. She has to make changes inch by inch, for now, even though her personality would really love to take life by the mile.

Dumbo and Me

Lasting change requires two things: a plan and the motivation to tackle it. In the fascinating book *Switch*, Chip and Dan Heath refer to these two parts of our decision-making brain as the Rider and the Elephant. The Rider is the planner, the logical part of us that researches, makes lists, and follows steps into change. The Elephant is that big, emotive part of ourselves that has to be reached and motivated to make a change, even a small one. An Elephant without a Rider is all feeling and impulse, lumbering and stampeding with heartfelt, unbridled, and directionless emotion. Still, the Elephant has its own kind of intuitive wisdom and needs to be heard and acknowledged.

The Rider without the Elephant, on the other hand, is like a woman standing on a path in the jungle, a well-thumbed guidebook in hand—but without the gumption needed to move off center and actually go somewhere. How many of us have embarked on a new diet or exercise plan, or determined to "get this house organized"—only to find our Inner Dumbo has decided to sit down and roll all over our best intentions? Perhaps dousing us with a spray of pond water for good measure? What happened? In short, we did not take the time needed to hear, get to know, and motivate our Inner Elephant.

Think back to a time in your life when you made a real change that lasted. You'll recognize that your Inner Elephant and your Rider were in sync, working together to get you down a new path that took your life's happiness quota up a few notches. Though I am naturally a messy person, I fell deeply in love with a good man who needs at least a modicum of order to feel balanced and happy. Motivated by love for my husband and a desire to see him functioning at his best (engaging the Elephant of feeling and motivation), I made a plan and put into action the steps of cleaning up the kitchen and living room every evening (the Rider) until they became natural habits. Our lives are happier for this relatively minor adjustment that eventually turned into a habit that I've kept up for almost a decade now.

One of the simple reasons that Rachel's extreme schedule makeover didn't work out (besides factors like illness and drop-in-crazy people) was that, frankly, she didn't give her Inner Elephant that much-desired cup of coffee. And that Elephant wasn't going to budge without caffeine, no matter how much her logical Inner Rider argued against it.

If you want to follow a lasting and nourishing way to change, you've got to make friends with your Inner Rider and Elephant.

Miracle Shifts in Perspective

Some of the most instantly freeing changes you make in your life will have nothing to do with a physical plan of action. They are simply decisions to shift your perspective or reframe a frustrating situation or minimize the impact some toxic person has on your life. This change involves nothing more than transforming your thoughts. And in fact, once you've "got your head in a better place"—it could be that nothing more is needed. I didn't need to cancel Thanksgiving ... but I did need to slow down and calm down and see life through the eyes of my grandchild for a few minutes. Maybe you don't need a new job, but a fresh attitude instead. Maybe you don't need to lose twenty pounds; you just need to love the body you are in and see it as sexy and gorgeous as is.

Most of the time, however, nourishing change involves a little of both—a little shift in perspective and a little action. A better attitude can keep you happy at your current job while still searching for a career that is a better, more enjoyable fit for you. Love and embrace your body as is; see it as womanly and beautiful, curvy, or voluptuous ... and then treat it with healthy food and enjoyable exercise and maybe lose three or four pounds—and that could be all you need to feel a whole lot happier in your own skin.

Imagine two good friends, one named Loving Acceptance, and one named Take Action walking toward each other, meeting each other halfway between their two homes for a friendly cup of coffee and conversation and hug. This middle is where most of the magic takes place. Where we cut ourselves a little mental slack, even as we simultaneously work toward a doable goal. We meet ourselves in the middle, adjusting our attitude, and making some actual tweaks or changes.

While I was writing this chapter, my husband and I flew to Tampa. A literary agent, he'd accepted an invitation to attend a conference and hear new writers pitch their books. The Hotel Vinoy in St. Petersburg, Florida, where the conference was held, was absolutely stunning. The bad news: the airline lost our luggage.

Greg and I automatically activated Loving Acceptance into the situation, alongside Take Action. He filled out the papers and made several calls to the airline, but neither of us let ourselves get upset about not having our suitcases. We were kind, rather than cranky, to the hotel clerk, who immediately took pity on us and upgraded our room. We could not believe it when we walked into our accommodations for the next three days. There was an enormous living room, a separate bedroom, a huge bathroom with a separate shower and tub, and not one, but two private porches. Sitting on one of the palm-tree-lined porches was a private Jacuzzi.

"Who needs clothes?" we both asked at about the same moment.

We chose to laugh, to make the best of it. I thought of myself as Elly May Clampett as I washed out the clothes we had on our backs, then laid them out in the sun near the Jacuzzi while we lounged in the fancy hotel robes. "Alright, Sugar," I said in my best *Beverly Hillbillies* twang, "now that I've done the washin', let's go for a dip in the cement pond and then head out to rustle us up some vittles."

The next morning I was grateful to find I'd packed lipstick, a bathing suit, and a pair of sunglasses in my carry-on. The sunglasses covered my mascara-and-liner-less eyes, and I was more than happy to spend the day in my bathing suit by the pool. The one thing I did not have was a comb, and there was not one to be found in the hotel. So I scrounged in my purse and found a couple of bobby pins, then twisted and piled the tangled mess of hair on top of my head and called it an "upsweep." When I walked back into the hotel room after a few hours of sunning, there was still no luggage, but on the table sat a beautiful tray with a bottle of chilled Clos du Bois Chardonnay, a basket of tasty snacks, and a note from our sweet hotel clerk saying, "I hope this helps compensate a little for your lost luggage. Enjoy!"

Greg and I had the most fun sipping wine as we enjoyed a little soak in our private Jacuzzi, feeling like King and Queen of the Hotel Vinoy. Twenty-four hours after our arrival, and a few phone calls to the airline later, our suitcases arrived, and there was much rejoicing in the kingdom. But the truth is, we were already rejoicing, having an absolute ball because we'd decided not to let a couple of missing suitcases ruin this special getaway together.

When Loving Acceptance (adjusting to what we can't change) meets Take Action (do what we can without working ourselves into a frenzy) — good stuff happens. We find ourselves feeling surprisingly nourished and happy. And life, I've noticed, also has a way of meeting our positive choices with surprising reinforcements of its own. If we had lost our luggage and not taken it in stride, we'd not have experienced a world-class hotel room, a Jacuzzi, or that lovely free bottle of wine. If we'd taken our frustrations out on the clerk, if we'd been cranky or rude, this story would have ended differently. If Greg or I had decided to get grumpy instead of getting in a romantic, playful mood, we could have ruined our time together.

So remember that change that will nourish your life

- needs to engage both your Rider and Elephant brain.
- needs to find a happy middle between (1) accepting what you can't change or don't want to change with a better

attitude, and (2) doing what you can, following through with diligence, but not crazed or cranky obsessiveness.

If all this sounds similar to the Serenity Prayer, well, it is. There's a reason this prayer is so popular. Anne Lamott calls it, "a Greatest Hits prayer."[4] It is brilliant and it works.

Nourishing Compromises

Though Rachel and I began writing this book thinking we'd come up with ways to radically change our lives, we quickly found that what works best in real life is learning the art of making nourishing compromises.

You'll see in the stories that unfold from here that change, for us, was often two steps forward and one back; that we'd sometimes have to pause and reevaluate our plan because it was obvious that our Elephant's heart was not really in it and, in fact, was in danger of rolling over on us. And sometimes it felt like God took our brilliant ideas from our hands and gently tossed them into a lake, even as He handed us new ones that turned out to be surprisingly better.

After some discussion, Rachel and I decided to begin our first experiment in nourishing change by focusing on getting our respective environments in order. We instinctively felt that if we could somehow get order and serenity around us, particularly in our homes, it would help usher in peace of mind.

What we didn't factor in was at least one major out-of-the-blue surprise ahead. And yes, I do feel like I've had more than my fair share of sudden surprises this year. *Really, God, I've got plenty of material. You can surprise somebody else now.*

PART 2

Nourished Spaces and Routines

Chapter 4

Does This Clutter Make My Brain Look Fried?

Nourishing Nests

Decorating is not about making stage sets,
it's not about making pretty pictures for the magazines;
it's really about creating a quality of life,
a beauty that nourishes the soul.
Albert Hadley

RACHEL

Clutter has always been Mom's calling card, whereas order has typically been my Prozac.

"Mom," I said as I rocked my then-baby Jackson to sleep in her living room, my eyes surveying the uber decorated surroundings. It looked less like a living room and more like an antique mall. "Please don't take this the wrong way, but sometimes less really is more."

"What do you mean?" she asked, peeking in from the connecting kitchen.

"I know you love all the cute old knickknacks that you and

Greg find on your estate sale jaunts, but you might want to consider leaving some blank spaces here and there on your walls, shelves, and ... floor. I really don't want to end up on the show *Hoarders*, having to bring in the therapists and county health agents to haul you and Greg out from under a pile of antique Christmas ornaments and vintage rolling pins."

"At least we don't have any pets," she said.

"Yet. All I can say is that it's a slippery slope from too much vintage clutter to becoming that lady with forty-seven cats."

If Mom's decorating style were a snow cone, it would be rainbow flavored. It's a little bit bohemian, a little bit eclectic, and a whole lot of vintage gone wild. Everything with Mom's decor is *more*. There is not one inch on her two-door refrigerator that isn't covered with magnets and pictures of kids and grandkids. Last time I was visiting, I caught her standing in her kitchen thoughtfully surveying the huge fridge collage, hoping she might be pondering a little thinning out of some snapshots. She finally said with a sigh, "If Greg and I have any more grandkids, we're going to have to buy another refrigerator."

This is the kind of Mother Logic I'm up against.

Perhaps it is not surprising, then, that my decorating preferences lean to more spacious than stuffed. My style would be more that of vanilla-cream snow cone, more "cottage chic" than "hippy chic." I like palettes of muted neutrals, natural wood tones, soft almost-greens, with touches of warm reds. Mom's favorite color combo is poppy red, hot tangerine, canary yellow, and eggplant purple. I want my space to say, "Sit, rest, have some tea, relax," while Mom wants her rooms to shout, "Fiesta!"

I like my surfaces mostly clean of clutter. Mom never met an empty surface she didn't think looked "sad and alone" and in need of some company.

And yet, for all my good intentions and the visions of serenity dancing in my head, I have to admit my house is stuck in limbo. My perfectionist tendencies paralyze me with indecision. Everything from what color to paint a bathroom wall, to which family photos to display, to how to store the multitude of mom-related purses and bags ... keep me stymied. My problem is the exact opposite of Mom's, with her tendency to dive in and overdo. While Mom puts anything that makes her happy up on her walls, I have been waiting two years now to find *the* perfect wall decor for each room in our house, which leaves me with a lot of bare "sad and lonely" spaces.

In fact, most of what now hangs on my walls came from two Christmases ago when my mom, who was staying the week with me, was about to go mad with all the white space. She took me to a home-decor store, gave me a hundred dollars, and stuck by my side until I spent every penny. Once home, she encouraged me to get out the ladder and hammer and hang up most of my pictures, which was wise of her, because the one painting we did not hang that day is still sitting on the floor of my office waiting for the right home. I have to admit that the space around my fireplace mantel where Mom and I secured a big clock and arranged some special knickknacks into a vignette is now one of my favorite spots in our home. All it took was a little tough-love shopping therapy.

During my pregnancy with Jackson, my perfectionist tendencies soared along with my hormones, rendering me nearly incapable of making decisions. After no less than ten visits to Lowe's for paint samples, our bedroom wall looked like an oversized artist's palette. Finally, after months of staring at the multihued wall, and driving myself nearly up it trying to pick the perfect color, I forced myself to choose one and get 'er done.

Mission accomplished, I decided to knock out the adjoining master bathroom while I was in the mood. I rolled on several strokes of a bluish-gray paint above my tub, to see how the color looked under bright vanity lights. At this point I realized much of the project would require a ladder (unsafe for a woman who was eight months with child, and/or a husband, and mine was working and traveling long hours). Then the baby was born, followed by a two-book contract, along with little things that once helped me function as a human: sleep, structure, and predictability. In short, my nesting phase took flight.

Which brings us to why, more than two years later, there is still a swatch of blue-gray paint, the size of my dining-room table, on the wall in my bathroom. It taunts me every time I soak in my garden tub. *Sure, soak away your troubles; I'll just be here looking down on you and your inability to finish a project.*

At this writing, I'm a mom to a two-year-old All-Boy Demolition Expert. The rhythm of our life is in constant flux due to the seasonal nature of my husband's coaching job. So the home decor I dreamed of is still ... well, mostly stuck in my dreams. Rather than a warm invitation to "Sit, relax, have some tea," my house offers more of a stressed-out apology. "Sorry about the obstacle course of toys and blankies. I'd offer you tea, but since it's stuffed out of reach on a top shelf, unless you're willing to let me stand on your shoulders for a moment, it's probably not going to happen."

I'm growing more desperate for a space where I can unwind and prop up my feet without unfinished projects literally looming over me. With football season approaching (when Jared is seldom home, and I am perpetually overwhelmed) and a busy writing and speaking season ahead, I am determined to find a way to bring order to our home.

One thought grew to an idea that resonated within me as truth: if Mom and I could start our journey to a more "nourishing life" by first getting a handle on our physical surroundings, then the clutter in our minds might begin to relax and order itself as well.

I picked up my phone and dialed, anxious to share my theory.

BECKY

My cell phone rang and I followed the sound to the fruit bowl, digging it out from beneath a ripening mango and a green banana.

It was Rachel, and I could tell she was on a mission. "Mom, I think we'll both feel more peaceful and even get more work done if we can get the spaces around us to feel more inspiring and functional. I know I tease you about your 'explosive' decorating style, but I've got my issues too. They're the opposite of yours, but in a way, they're related. You get sidetracked with the hundreds of pretty and interesting things, and I'm paralyzed by perfection. Different brain challenges, but we're both stuck in ruts."

As I listened to Rachel while holding the phone with one hand, I used my free hand to open the fridge to grab a pitcher of tea, but instead a quart jar of mayonnaise rolled out and landed on my foot.

"I know you're right, Rachel. But where do we even begin?" I asked, rubbing my aching instep as I chased the roving mayo around the floor. The irony did not escape me. This was my life. I reach for one thing and end up bruised and confused, chasing something totally unrelated to my original goal — all because my life and my home, like my fridge, are overstuffed.

I've been a messy as long as I can remember. As a young teen, when someone in my family couldn't find an item the conversation that proceeded was inevitable: "Where is … [insert: my baseball bat? my hair brush? the banana I was just eating]?" In unison the reply would be, "Check under Becky's bed!" All rivers of missing paraphernalia culminated in the ocean of stuff under my bed. We can't explain why. It is a mystery, like black holes and Einstein's hair.

Returning to the conversation at hand, I said, "You know, Rach, though it's definitely not working for me right now, I do think the ability to live cheerfully in disorder probably served me well when you and your brothers were young."

My mind flashed to the days when our family of six all lived in an 865-square-foot cabin in the country on the bank of a fishing lake. My youngest son, Gabe, at age four, especially loved collecting reptiles and amphibians and would leave them randomly around the house or in the station wagon. Frequently, I'd drive down the road and feel a turtle nudge my toe or a frog hop up on my shoulder. It hardly fazed me.

Rachel agreed. "I know raising four kids in a small cabin was a challenge all its own, Mom. Then add to that the hazards of country living. Do you remember the time that family of possums decided to live in our laundry room?"

"Gosh, yes! Mean little boogers. Sharp teeth. But if you ever have to wash clothes in the wild, you'll know how to outmaneuver small menacing animals. Well, our home life was crazy, but it sure gave me a lot of comic material for the books I was writing."

"And plenty of stories to tell a therapist, if I ever need one," Rachel quipped.

"Oh, Rach," I sighed, "our life was anything but neat and normal. I sometimes wonder how we survived. Especially since you craved order. But there were good times, and it seemed our house was always filled with kids who loved coming to a place they truly couldn't mess up."

"True, true," Rachel said, laughing. Then, thoughtfully, she added, "I do realize, now that I'm a mom, there's no way I can have a perfectly clean home all the time and still enjoy Jackson and let him be a child. But this feeling of my house being 'on hold' makes me feel like I'm stuck in some emotional waiting room."

"I know you'll find a balance that will work for you. Once you get your mind set on something, you do it. I'll admit, I'm also ready to do some decluttering."

RACHEL

I hung up the phone, sat down on the couch, and put my feet up. Jackson was napping, and my thoughts drifted back to my childhood again, where my desire for perfect order probably began to take root. In the middle of all my brothers and the critters and mess and craziness, I stood as the lone daughter, wide-eyed and taking notes in my mental organizer of the sort of home I did and did not want someday. My bedroom was the only real refuge from the nuttiness of the house. (My dad—an active, never-sit-still kind of guy—refused to build "boring old stairs" to the second story, so I had to climb either the ladder, the rope, or the rock-climbing wall to get there.) Mom and Dad and my big brother, Zeke, helped me paint my room and furniture girly shades of pink, silver, and white. I organized my wardrobe by season and then color, my dirty laundry in three separate bins (darks, lights, and whites), and my schoolwork by subject and date. I dreamed of the day when I'd be in charge of a whole house where order could reign in every room; where the outdoors would stay put out-of-doors; where I'd never have to be on guard against a possum or a snapping turtle to simply access the laundry room and iron a shirt.

Now that I have just one child of my own, and nearly three thousand square feet of home (a bargain foreclosure in a small town), two working bathrooms, a dishwasher, a dryer, and a fifty-gallon hot-water heater, I have a lot more empathy for the challenges my mother had to face every day. If I struggle to keep our home in order for a small family of three, I can only imagine the challenges she faced with old used appliances that malfunctioned more than they functioned, a tiny hot-water heater that barely heated water for one bath (that is, when we finally traded in the portable shower stall for a real bathtub-shower combo), and four kids with wildly different schedules. All this while simultaneously trying to get her degree and come up with a way to contribute to the family budget. She did her best to raise four kids in a cabin on little more than love and laughter.

I reached over and picked up a book I'd recently purchased by Peter Walsh, *Does This Clutter Make My Butt Look Fat?* (I bought it mostly because the title made me laugh.) My eyes landed on this sentence: "Clutter gets in the way of living the life you want. It makes it hard to breathe. It makes it hard to move. It makes it hard to see clearly. It makes it hard to focus and stay motivated. You have to clean outside to get clean inside."[5]

The current state of my home was anything but calm. There were pockets of order, however, and it was interesting to note that in rooms where I did activities I loved, order seemed to reign. I highly value my cooking time, so my kitchen is decorated, organized, and clean 90 percent of the time. Jackson's room too is well-organized, decorated, and functional—because his routines and sleep are a high priority for me. Sadly, our bedroom is still half-finished, and I wonder if that says something about needing to put myself and my marriage a little higher on the priority list. I obviously value my child's sleep haven more than our own.

I looked around the house, as if I were not its owner but a professional organizer, taking note of the rooms that need SOS help: our master bedroom, my office, the entryway, and our bathroom.

My motivation is high. My Inner Rider is making lists of changes I plan to make and hopping on my emotional Elephant, who is trumpeting, "Wow! This sounds *fun!*"

We're ready to push through the jungle of clutter.

BECKY

To keep my sanity during the years of living in the country in tiny quarters with lots of kids, I determined to look at my life through Erma Bombeck eyes, as if my life were an unfolding sitcom, jotting down anecdotes to entertain friends and family. It helped. We laughed a lot. But I also cried quite a bit, behind the scenes. The disorder in my life then, within and without, took its own kind of personal toll.

Fast-forward twenty years. I am now living in a six-bedroom spacious home in a nice suburb of Denver. My backyard is professionally landscaped with a privacy fence around it. My husband, Greg, and I have been married for a decade, and in those years I have come a looooong way, baby, in terms of cleanliness and order. May I just say how much it helps to have running water, central heat and air, no children, plenty of bathrooms, and an actual set of real stairs to the second story? Throw in a naturally neat husband who offices at home, never leaves so much as a sock on the floor, regularly helps with the dishes and sweeping, and immediately tends to any items in need of repair, and I have to admit, the care and keeping of a tidy house is eons easier.

Even though my grown children will tell you I've tremendously improved in my general tidiness, I'm still "Becky," and that means I still have my areas of struggle. In the last few years, after working alongside a couple of brain specialists on writing projects, I discovered that I have "inattentive ADD," which means that I can focus on something that is highly absorbing and interesting to me, even if the ceiling should fall down around me. This ability came in handy when I was writing books in a small cabin surrounded by four noisy kids and a handful of squirmy critters. This ability is both gift and handicap and often the source of amazed amusement from others.

Not long ago I was in the kitchen fully focused on creating a new recipe. Something had fallen at my feet, but I didn't even glance down to see what it was. Greg watched me stepping over it deftly several times, my eyes glued to the skillet in front of me. After watching and waiting a few seconds to see if I'd look down and pick it up, he asked, incredulously, "Becky, did you know there is a whole pineapple on the floor that you've been walking around and over?" No. Clue.

When Georgie was getting used to living with us, discovering the lay of the land as it were, he opened my freezer, surveyed the contents of bags and boxes that I'd haphazardly stuffed in, and asked, "Nonny, is this another place where you keeps your trash?"

He started a morning routine of coming into our room, hopping on my bed, and playing, "What's in Nonny's nest?" Giggling, he'd hand me all the things he found on my side of the bed in and around and under the covers: cell phone, laptop, Nook, glasses, pens, notepads, hair clips, books, earrings, TV remote, power bars … are just a few of the items he finds on a regular basis. I've always found a measure of comfort in having lots of stuff around me when I sleep, like a pack rat's nest.

I could list dozens of areas where I fight the tide of disorganization, but few have been as daunting as keeping pills, vitamins, and supplements in their bottles, something that unnerves both Rachel and Greg. We have several spots in the house where miscellaneous pills and supplements have spilled then mingled together, like jelly bean assortments. I always plan on sorting them out, one day, looking up the embedded numbers on the internet to figure out if a mystery pill is an Aspirin or Gingko or rogue cyanide. The other night Greg asked if I had a Tylenol in my bedside table. I opened the drawer and took a dubious look at the pharmaceutical collage rolling about and asked, "Are you feelin' lucky?"

"Never mind," he said. "I'm not brave enough for Vitamin Roulette tonight."

He always double-checks, even when I give him a pill from a bottle, since the night I accidentally gave him a NoDoz instead of a sleep aid—a night he recalls every moment of in vivid detail. My purse is another interesting place where pills and vitamins like to gather and do odd things. Rachel and Jackson were recently here visiting, and the adjustment to the altitude gave her a nasty migraine. "Do you have an Excedrin, Mom?" she asked as she rubbed her head.

"Just a minute," I said, digging in my purse. "Ah-ha! I do! Here you go."

She took the pill, and a puzzled look crossed her face. "Mom, that's a red M&M."

"No, honey. See the E on the front? It's 'Excedrin.'"

"Mom, put on your reading glasses. See, you've got 'the pill' rotated the wrong way. Give it a quarter turn. See? It's an M, and there's a little chocolate showing where the red candy has melted in your purse and is now melting in my hands."

"My goodness, I've kept those three M&Ms in the zipper pocket of my purse for two months, sure they were painkillers. Whaddaya know?"

All this preamble is to say, though I am much improved from my days as a teen and young mom—I still struggle. Organization is as sticky a subject as the console of my car.

I do, however, have a few good organizational habits spinning. As I mentioned earlier, Greg is laid-back about some areas of the house, but he needs order in a few of the main shared areas. Once I developed the habit of always cleaning the kitchen at night and, if possible, leaving no dishes in the sink, he also encouraged me in the habit of emptying my car every time I park and come into our home. He placed a big trash can by the back door in the garage, and without even thinking about it, I now autogather trash and toss it in the can every time I enter the house. Brilliant.

Still the truth is ... I am mostly a messy. About 70 percent more Oscar Madison than Felix Unger. I wanted to change; I really did. I remember hearing someone on some radio show say, "Messy people often don't really value themselves enough to keep their surroundings clean and neat. They don't think they are worth the trouble."

Gulp.

What if that were true?

If we really loved and valued ourselves, would we learn to better prioritize the serenity in our personal spaces? Was I too buried under clutter to see a more nourishing way to live in our home? I see in my husband how his little daily habits of preparation keep his mind at ease and his life running smoothly. Because he sets the timer on the coffee pot each evening, he gets to wake up to the smell of brewing java; because he hangs up and folds his fresh laundry right away, he actually has clean underwear and socks available to him 24/7 without having to search through mounds of clothes, unsure of what's clean or dirty. He calls this "being kind to his future self." He juggles hundreds of clients' work projects, a mind-boggling task for the most detailed person. Part of the reason he is a natural at being an agent is that he actually gets a kick out of organizing and often does it—get this—*for fun*. (He was, apparently, born with an Elephant that has a natural jones for organizing.)

I determined to be a little more like Greg and a little less like Messy Me.

In my mind—and on various notepads that I've lost and found about a dozen times—I formulated a *plan*: a long-term, slowgoing, home-and-garden improvement, get-it-together-and-organize-my-house *plan*.

And then, suddenly, something happened. It was as if God saw my addicted-to-chaos condition and said, "Forget her plan. This little gal needs an extreme makeover. She will not change without going cold turkey on clutter, and I know just how to make this happen."

And let me tell you, I would need all the Red Bull for the soul that God could give me to accomplish what came next.

Chapter 5

Home Sweet
Uncluttered Home

Nourishing Places
and Welcoming Spaces

As much as we need to go out into the world to explore,
we are that much braver and confident when we know that
we have a place of sanctuary that will welcome us back from
the adventure.... Creating a nurturing, nourishing home
is a process that is always unfolding in its own perfect way.
Leah Kent

BECKY

So here's what landed, out of the blue, to change our living environment almost overnight: we decided to sell our home and get it ready for showing. In less than ten days. At this writing, I've been to intensive decluttering boot camp beyond anything I could imagine and have a stack of sweaty T-shirts to prove it.

A call from a realtor brought me to this extreme *Designed to Sell* makeover experience. It all began innocently enough. I happened upon a pretty house for sale, closer to our adult kids and grandkids in southwest Denver. It overlooked a creek, a serene pond with ducks, and a cute park. I could just see our five grandsons having

57

so much fun playing in Nonny and Poppy's backyard if we were to somehow find a way to buy this home. To our surprise the owner agreed to a contingency contract. The catch was this: we had to get our house on the market in ten days and sell it first. The realtor sent over a professional stager who, with a straight face, serenely informed us that we'd need to remove half our furniture and all our clutter along with any personal photos, then give our place a fresh coat of paint, do lots of repairs, and decorate it stylishly and sparsely—like a hotel. New tile would have to be laid in the master bathroom where I had dyed my hair and much of the carpet with L'Oréal Bronzed Brown #51. And it needed to be done in a week and a half, as time was a-tickin'!

That's a lot of work for any able-bodied couple to tackle in a short time, and we are middle-aged with "barely able" bodies-on-the-soft-side. But here's the real kicker: Greg was gone five out of those ten days on a business trip. The night he came home from said trip, already fatigued from lack of sleep, he caught an evil virus and spent the next twenty-four hours emptying the contents of his stomach. It took two days for him to heal enough to walk among the living again. So he was either absent or nonfunctional for eight out of the ten crucial "extreme home makeover" days. I took care of him the best I could between packing boxes, moving furniture, and cleaning like a madwoman. The role reversal was sudden and ... disorienting.

At the beginning of the task, I felt a surprising rush of adrenaline. It was challenging, even invigorating, to find myself the Woman in Charge of a Big Project. In some ways it was like being a contestant on some kind of survivor reality show. I'd never worked that hard from dawn to dark, physically, for days on end. Every night I would wake up with muscle spasms, rising in the wee hours to take a hot bath and painkillers to get back to sleep. Morning seemed to come so very, very early. Bedtime so very, very late. Georgie observed me one day with concern and asked,

"Nonny, why are you talking like an oooold woman and moving like you's bones are rusty?"

Some bright TV producer needs to throw away the treadmills and barbells on *The Biggest Loser* and combine their show, instead, with HGTV's *Designed to Sell*. Put people who want to lose weight and get in shape in charge of cleaning out the houses of messy midlife nesters who love to collect things. Make sure there are a lot of stairs. Then give them a paintbrush and an active boy to keep an eye on, and set a timer to see how fast they can paint a bedroom before the six-year-old touches a wet wall or steps in the paint can.

By the time it was all said and done, the ten days up, and the house ready for its first "showing," Greg and I had to leave together on a business trip to California. I felt and looked like a lab rat who'd been deprived of sleep for ten days and made to run on a wheel without stopping. My motto has always been "one day at a time," but my fragile condition was the result of several days attacking me at once.

I sat in the front seat of the car as Greg drove to the airport. He reached over to hold my hand as I dripped tears, a leaky faucet, all the way there. "I don't know why I'm crying," I said, as the tears continued to fall. I was exhausted in every way a woman can be drained, especially because of who I had become at the end of ten intense days of getting my house from Messy Nest to House Beautiful. I'd turned into a type-A, hyperpicky, cranky person. I couldn't abide this personality, and yet it seemed the requirement for keeping a perfect home in constant show condition.

The next morning was the first time in ten days that I was able to move at my leisure. Greg and I gazed at each other in wonder, as if seeing one another for the first time in two weeks.

We took a little walk on a beach near our hotel after a leisurely breakfast, and I noticed something strange. After my *Designed to Sell* workout, walking suddenly felt so easy that for the first time in our married life I told Greg that I'd like to walk a little faster, rather than begging him to slow down.

We returned home and kept up the craziness for two more weeks, showing our house one to two times a day. And then I hit a wall. Well, actually to be more precise: my backside hit a cart.

I was standing in line to buy one more decorative item at Home Depot to "help our house sell," when I, in a constant state of hurry, backed up to move to a shorter line. Only I did not realize there was a low-riding flatbed cart behind me. It snagged me right under my calves, and I fell straight back like a plank, until I found myself lying on bags of mulch and looking up at the warehouse ceiling. A man in a bright orange apron came into focus, asking me if I was okay. Other than a half-dozen bruises, a few scrapes, and complete loss of dignity, I was fine. Just *fine*.

Lying flat on that Home Depot cart, face up, initiated a sudden and strong epiphany. As I limped to my car in the giant parking lot, bleeding from one ankle, I picked up my cell phone and called my husband. "We have to stop the madness. My first book with Rachel is debuting this summer, and it will likely be the last few months of getting to have our grandson live with us. I want to be fully present in my own head for both of these special seasons. I'm going to either break my leg or my brain if I keep going at this pace."

"Done," Greg said.

"Really?" I asked.

"We'll take the house off the market tomorrow."

The moment he said this, I relaxed. Once home, I looked around and immediately began refalling in love with my house. The back porch had never looked so beautiful. Summer had greened the grass and trees; colorful flowers were in full bloom. When I sat on the porch swing surveying my gardenlike yard, I could not believe I'd ever thought of moving. This house was *perfect*. With fresh paint, decluttering, a good cleaning, and a little decorating, my home seemed to beckon, "Welcome! Stay awhile longer, won't you?"

This little month-long saga cost us a pretty penny and enormous amounts of time and energy. I'm trying hard to see it as a major spring cleaning and shape-up plan (instead of a plot only Dumb and Dumber could have dreamed up). I broke some bad habits and gained some better ones. Some people would pay good money for these training lessons, I suspect. Now, though I'm going at a more relaxed pace, I'm continuing the "get up early, and speed clean the house" exercise routine, and not only is my house continuing to get more and more ordered, my body is getting more and more fit. My jeans are loose for the first time in years. It's double motivation: I'm losing weight and loving the order and beauty of my home. Who knew my own home, and the cleaning thereof, was equal to or even superior to a gym?

Here are some ideas you may want to try to get you started on your own extreme house makeover, without the hassle of actually putting your house on the market for a month.

1. Begin by getting a room "show ready" on the surface. Don't worry right away about what's behind cabinets and in drawers. The serenity of getting one room at a time, and eventually the whole house, surface-beautiful—in a short amount of time—is highly motivating.

2. Because it is both time-consuming and instantly rewarding, after surface cleaning, I suggest starting the reorganizing makeover in your closet. Use pretty baskets or see-through boxes to organize items on your shelves. In addition to a dirty-clothes hamper, designate one basket for "Clothes to Hang Up or Put Away" and one for "To Be Mended" with a sewing kit tucked inside. Under-the-bed storage containers work great for out-of-season clothing.

3. Clear counters, bedside tables, and surfaces of all stuff, including decorations. Then decide what you really need.

If it can be put in a decorative hinged box or basket, consider that. I bought pretty cozies for Kleenex boxes, pretty boxes for lotions and reading glasses, baskets for books, plastic containers for laundry supplies. It surprised me how containing miscellaneous items in attractive ways instantly adds to the neat appearance of a room.

4. Thrift stores can be such great friends! I found almost all of the decorative baskets, containers, linens, lamps, artwork, and vases for our home makeover at thrift stores. Drop off items you don't need, and save on items that actually add to the functionality of your home—a decluttering dream!

5. When the house is surface clean and decorated, and your clothes closet is looking neat, start again at your leisure and organize one drawer and one cabinet per day. For a messy like me, beautifying (the fun part) leads to and gives motivation to declutter (the not-fun part). I found myself looking for excuses to linger in my newly spruced spaces, so cleaning out a drawer gave me a reason to stay and bask in the beauty awhile.

6. If you are doing a quick pickup of the house, grab a lightweight laundry basket to take with you from room to room so you can carry things back to their "home" easily. Also try cleaning around the room in order so you don't waste steps going back and forth willy-nilly. Because willy-nilly is just plain silly.

Feeling Lighter

I have realized that in letting go of stuff, I am also letting go of so many other things that weigh me down, besides a few pounds. The mental stress that comes with opening a messy drawer or looking everywhere for a needed item adds up in the toll it takes on our psyches. On the other hand, the brain-freeing "ahhhhh" that comes with starting the day with a fresh clean house, the bed made, the dishwasher humming, laundry in manageable cycles, is a surprising joy to me. I once saw housekeeping as a time stealer. Now I'm beginning to see it as a way to get my body moving first thing in the morning, and—to everyone's shock and awe—I'm becoming just a wee bit addicted to having everything in order. A basically clean space frees up mental space for me to sit down to write or whatever tasks await me each day.

I am not going to become type A, because nobody can stand me in that mode, especially myself. But I'm not comfortable living in a messy nest anymore either. I think I may be finding my unique balance between two extremes. Pearl Buck wrote, "Order is the shape upon which beauty depends." I've always been a fan of beauty, not so much order, as it seemed so impossible for my personality type to achieve. Let's be realistic, even at my most neat, I am probably still messier than most. But I'm finding my way toward more order, and therefore, more relaxed beauty in the spaces around me.

RACHEL

Slow and Steady Alternate House Beautiful *Plan*

Needless to say, I found it fascinating to watch my mom and her house transform in such a short time. In the reversal of all reversals, who would have thought *Mom* might motivate *me* to get my house act together?

While Mom was pushed to an extreme home do-over all at once, I'm in a place of having to eat this house-organization elephant one bite at a time. As much as my get-'er-done persona would love to take ten days to do a whole house makeover, my work schedule, bank account, and toddler didn't allow me the opportunity. Even so, I've made lots of small changes over the last few months that add up to a big change in how I feel about my house.

The first nourishing change I made was to block out a few hours and designated days for guilt-free cleaning and organizing. Before my epiphany that an orderly house equals an orderly life, I felt that cleaning or organizing during Jackson's naps was a waste of good writing time. What I discovered, though, was that allowing myself one or two days a week to clean and organize, without feeling guilty about the writing work waiting for me, energized me for days. When I did sit down to write, I found I worked more efficiently in my new calm surroundings. (And Jackson played more independently in his, freeing me up even more.) Setting aside specific times and days for cleaning and organizing lowered my stress levels in other surprising ways. I could look at a mess and say to myself, "Today is a work/writing day, but tomorrow I can let work go and get the house back in order." In the beginning, I gave myself two days a week to devote to Operation Get My House in Order, but now that the hard work is done, it takes only an hour or two once a week to get the house in shape.

Here are the epiphanies I found most helpful in my own slower-paced, but remarkably helpful home makeover.

1. Designate a catchall room

There were several spaces in my house I felt inspired to address right away—and other areas (for instance, filing mounds of paper) that I didn't have the brain energy or the "want to" to tackle yet. Designating one catchall place "to be dealt with later" helped tremendously in my house makeover. I rarely use my actual office to work in, so I assigned it as the catchall room. Items to sell, sort, file, or store went into the office, so I didn't have to stop the momentum of the makeover on the rest of the house. This gave me immediate gratification when I finished a room—no looming piles to work through before I could relax in a newly beautified space.

Now that the rest of the house is mostly in order, I can spend thirty minutes here and there sorting through piles in the catchall room. If you don't have an extra room, you can clear out a space in your garage or a closet as your catchall space. Because I want to use this room as a nursery for our second child someday, I've told myself, "I can't have another baby until it is clean." You may also want to give yourself a deadline to get your catchall room cleared up so it doesn't remain in permanent limbo. (Before relatives arrive, before Thanksgiving, before the kids go back to school, before the next Ice Age, and so on.)

2. Pamper yourself with nourishing nooks

Once you've done a "clean sweep," organize an area that will nourish your spirit. Creating these areas feels like small blessings you give yourself that keep on giving. I adopted Mom's plan of doing an overall clean sweep of the surface areas, then went back through my house to slowly address drawers and cabinets and deep cleaning. Of all the areas I've beautified, organized, and functionalized, one of my favorite makeovers is what I now call my tea drawer. I love a cup of tea, the feel of a warm mug in my hand, the fragrance of jasmine or Earl Grey. But for some reason, I'd been storing miscellaneous bags of tea up high on an almost inaccessible shelf, making it a royal pain to brew a simple cup of royal chai. Then came the idea to turn the drawer (near my coffeemaker and mugs and teacups) into a pretty tea drawer. I organized it into sections: caffeinated, decaf, loose tea. It was a small task, but every day the payoff to my mood feels like a luxurious indulgence.

"Would you like anything to drink?" I now ask my guests with a smile, showcasing my lovely beverage corner with a Vanna White flourish, opening the tea drawer as I glide my hand in the air across it. "Mugs are in the cabinet above, and the sugar bowl is here if you need it." The best part: I now often sit, relax, and sip a cuppa tea in my freshly put-together, calm, serene space.

I found an overlooked stack of books that I wanted to read, so I placed a decorative wire basket near the couch and filled it with reading material. Now, when Jackson is playing happily or my husband is watching a ball game, a good book is always within arm's reach.

Another nourishing nook I created was a sitting area in our bedroom. In an unused space in the corner, I placed a rocking chair and a secretary desk upon which I arranged my jewelry box, a Parisian-style sign that beckons a flirty *"Amour,"* and a special jar of feathers I've collected over the years. An old coatrack worked perfect for draping my favorite pretty scarves and hats on. The final touch: a cheval mirror. It's functional, beautiful, and adds warmth, personality, and a touch of French-style romance to our bedroom.

These little nourishing nooks didn't take much effort and cost me nothing, but they make me happy every time I see them.

3. No mudroom? Try a mud-hutch!

I never really understood why every issue of *Better Homes & Gardens* featured at least one perfectly organized mudroom with cute little monogrammed backpacks hanging on custom knobs and boots (sans any actual mud) stored below. Here in Texas, at least, I almost never see a house with an actual built-in mudroom.

One day, however, I realized that our dining room was basically functioning as a mudroom. My husband always emptied his pockets and piled up his collection of ball caps on the dining-room table, and his shoes adorned the dining-room floor. Then we had a baby. Have mercy. The snacks, the extra changes of clothes, the hats and the sunscreen, the diapers and wipes and Pull-Ups. And don't even get me started on the diaper bags themselves—the daddy bag, the school bag, the short-trip bag, the long-outing bag. I suddenly understood the need and desire for a mudroom ... but again, who has room for one?

Then a friend posted a big beautiful antique wooden hutch on a for-sale site for an unbeatable price. It proved to be the answer to everything that ailed me. We picked it up the next day and put it in our dining room. I got to work right away, turning it into our very own mudroom. Behind the two big doors and on the three spacious shelves, I added containers to hold all the coming-and-going accessories — snacks, diapers and wipes, toys and activities for car trips or restaurants, pool supplies, even a small trash can for quickly tossing out the junk mail. On the bottom shelf, a woven basket holds shoes. When I come home now, I immediately empty out the bag of choice — extra snacks go back into the snack box, toys into the toy box, and so on. Then when I leave again, I pack exactly what I need for the next outing with child in tow. Works like a *dream*.

You could do the same thing by customizing your "comings and goings" needs inside linen-closet shelves or a bookshelf with cute baskets. Mom has her own version of a "mudroom" too. She uses a basket by the front door for shoes, a hall tree for jackets and purses, and a picnic-sized basket on a hall bench that she fills with library books, items to return, or packages to mail — to take to and from the car.

4. Create flexible work zones

Because I often write at home, I need a *place* to write. In fact, ideally, I like to have a few places to work, depending on my mood and my son's schedule. It turns out, in the three homes we've lived in since Jared and I married, I always set up a cute little office for myself. And I've never enjoyed working in them. When I go into my home office, work suddenly feels like, ugh, *work*... and I fight it with every fiber in me. So I moved an extra desk into a corner of the living room as the central hub for my laptop and family/work calendar. And now, when I'm home, I never have to "go" to work!

To create another workspace, I moved the unused desk from

my "old office" into the guest room. I now have a place where I can shut the door and work if someone is watching Jackson for me in the bigger living areas. The guest room feels homey instead of officey, too, which for some reason makes my Inner Elephant happier.

For a long time I thought if I didn't sit down and work at a real desk with a swivel chair, I failed to show how serious I was about my writing career. But I was so wrong. I'm much more productive now that I've embraced my new kinder, gentler, homier work zones and said goodbye to "going to work" in a room with no function other than being an office.

Whether you need a place to work in your home, an area to pay bills, a place to craft, or simply a quiet place to sit and be with God, consider setting up your work, hobby, or quiet place zones in areas that call your name and inspire you to be there.

5. Corral the kiddie clutter

When I was pregnant, I spent hours reading reviews on all-natural, neutral-toned toys and accessories for Jackson. The idea of bright primary colors and battery-operated noisemakers mixing into our decor, bleeping and buzzing into my quiet surroundings, turned my stomach to knots. But it didn't take long to realize that the crinkly, brightly colored plastic book entertains a baby twice as long as the organic wooden rattle. The trade-off for allowing those bright tacky-looking toys into my house is free time, precious moments of bliss when my child's focus is on something other than his need for my attention.

However, I've found a few tricks to keep our living room from looking as though it's been decorated by Disney. I indulge my taste for neutral, soothing color choices in the bigger storage and play items. Ikea, for example, has cheap wood-toned pint-sized tables and chairs and storage units. Or make your own by upcycling old nightstands or entertainment centers. Look for furniture with drawers, solid doors, and hidden storage. We tuck toys behind cabinet doors, in a bench, and in the TV stand. Crafts go in a kitchen cabinet, balls in a canvas basket on a shelf. Instead of a toy box (where toys go to get tangled, lose their parts, and often are never heard from again) — try grouping like items in open containers (like canvas totes) or cubbies. This also helps children understand organization and makes it easier for them to help clean up. I also rotate toys, putting away toys Jackson seems to have lost interest in, then trading it back into use awhile later. This way it almost feels like a new toy to him.

One night after I had the house mostly in order, Jackson helped me finish cleaning up his toys. He was having so much fun, he thought it was a game. "More clean, please?" he asked.

"Honey, we don't have anything else to clean," I told him. The house really was immaculate for maybe the first time in his life. "You'll have to mess something up if you want to clean more." Needless to say, he was happy to oblige.

I'd been blaming the obligations of motherhood for my messy life, and as it turned out, my two-year-old child was more than happy to help out with cleanup and order. All it took was some thought and time to create a home for every toy and to show him how and where to put them away.

Nourishing Compromises in Our Homes

Because real people live in them, our homes will always be works in progress. But now that I have a plan for future projects and have put organizing days on the calendar, I don't feel nearly as overwhelmed when I see unfinished projects around me.

At this writing, the gray-blue splotch of paint still adorns my bathroom wall. But because I have circled the week on my calendar when I plan to tackle this project, I have peace of mind. (Postscript: After two days of teetering on a ladder in the shower, crouching and reaching around the toilet, balancing on counter tops ... every inch of my master bathroom is painted. Whoever said painting is the easiest way to brighten a room was wrong, or didn't have ten-foot ceilings above their shower. Nevertheless, it was *so* worth the trouble. With one thirty-dollar can of paint, my bathroom finally feels like my own spa getaway.)

When you look at your home, how do you feel? Do you exhale and relax, soaking in your blessings? Do you want to invite someone over for a cup of tea or coffee? A warm, inviting home doesn't have to be a perfectly ordered home. It is just one that says, I value myself, I value my family, and I value relationships. Basically, when you walk into a nourishing home it feels like you're walking into a hug.

Whether you are doing a home makeover in ten days or gradually upgrading your home over the next year, putting some time and energy into your home will not only nourish you, but your family and friends who come into your space. Which in my case looks like me inviting a friend inside to put her feet up while I make her a cup of tea (from my handy-dandy tea drawer) and Jackson pulls a rainbow of noisy toys out from hiding behind the pretty wood cabinet.

Because, as my mom has always told me, no matter how organized we are, some of the best parts of real life (especially with kids) will always be messy. It's that nourishing compromise thing: order what you can; let go of what you can't control. The goal is to create a space where real families live and make messes but are simple to put right again at the end of the day.

Chapter 6

I Washed and Dried My Day Planner

Nourishing Schedules and Balanced Rhythms

Usually, when the distractions of daily life deplete
our energy, the first thing we eliminate
is the thing we need the most: quiet, reflective time.
Time to dream, time to contemplate what's working and
what's not, so that we can make changes for the better.
Sarah Ban Breathnach

RACHEL

After several cold, rainy days in October, the clouds parted and the sun came out just long enough to get together with a few friends and our kids at a petting zoo on a family farm out in the country. The morning was exactly what Jackson and I needed after being cooped up in the house for days. So when his nap time approached, I decided to linger a little longer. He was having such a good time, and I was getting to know a new friend over buckets of feed and baby goats nibbling at our kneecaps. Then the rain reappeared and poured on our playdate.

We took cover until there was a break in the clouds and then grabbed our kids to head home. Mine had made his way to the far side of the play area, on the opposite side from the zoo's exit. I said my goodbyes to friends and marched across the now freshly soggy farm. "It's time to go, buddy," I said, reaching out for his hand.

"I don't waaaaaant to goooooo!" he whined, walking backward out of my arm's reach.

"I know," I empathized. "It's hard to leave fun places, but we stayed extra long and now we need to get home before it rains again."

I feared we may have missed the window, the window in which you see your toddler yawning and starting to get a little fussy. In the window, you can scoop them up and carry them to bed or load them in the car with their blanky. There may be a little whining, but it's manageable.

"Nooooooo! I *stayyy!*" Jackson screamed, turning to run from me. Uh-oh. That small open window of his sanity had slammed shut. Now I faced a toddler in meltdown. I quickly scooped him up and carried him across the petting zoo as he screamed and cried and kicked his muddy boots all over me.

It was the first time he'd behaved poorly in public, and I was not taking it well. "Stand right there," I ordered, setting him down on the gravel parking lot, near the car. "Do *not* move an inch." I reached inside the open door to grab baby wipes to give him a quick wipe down. When I turned around to clean him off, I saw he'd made a break for it. He was running, like an escaped convict, as fast as he could through the (thankfully mostly empty) parking lot. My sharp-eyed, fast-footed two-year-old spotted a back entrance to the zoo I didn't even know existed. I followed in hot pursuit, but by the time I'd made it through the gate, he'd positioned himself on the opposite side of a muddy round pen meant for horses. (By God's grace, also empty.) Across the rusty red bar of the pen, he was staring me down with the iron will of a ... well, of a defiant, exhausted toddler.

I darted to the right to grab him. He matched my steps. I slowly paced to the left. Across the pen, keeping steady eye contact with me, like a cowboy ready for a draw, he paced right with me. A few rounds of this and I realized, checkmate, he had me. I could not get to him. Unless ...

I could make him fall.

I walked to the left, and he followed my lead, straight into a muddy patch. His pace slowed as his boots sank down into the muck. I quickly jabbed to the right. He jabbed too, but his feet didn't follow, and he fell right into my muddy trap.

His strong-willed defiance turned to a whimpering plea for his mommy.

This mom had lived to outsmart her toddler one more day. But no doubt about it, he'd proved a worthy opponent.

Plans (or Lack Thereof) That Push Our Limits

I've been there myself, metaphorically lying face up in the mud, exhausted, and crying uncle. I often allow my schedule to push me beyond my own window of sanity, leaving no margin for mishaps or divine interruptions ... or a nap. Though I sometimes overschedule days, more often my days unravel because I failed to make a clear plan at all. I woke up thinking, "I'll somehow get things done." But the day, like a willful toddler, most often escapes me. I don't even know where I'm going; I'm just trying to make a run for it, jabbing back and forth between tasks, frantically trying to get somewhere while my boots (or brain) are stuck someplace else. Really I'm just running in circles, getting splashed with the mud of overwhelm. At the end of the day, I'm left wondering, "What the heck just happened?"

From the way we start our day to how we plan our weeks, how we balance our activities and rest will determine how fulfilled (or frazzled) we are at the end of the day. Because everyone is different, one person's fulfilled day may leave another feeling anemic and overwhelmed. We want to fill in our calendar with activities that bring out the best in us with all our unique talents and limitations. In other words, we want to design a life schedule that nourishes us.

Since time is a limited resource, I found it a good idea to start my search for a more nourishing schedule by determining my real priorities. Otherwise, life itself was going to run away with my schedule and do it for me. And we all know where that can end up.

Clarify What Matters Most

So I sat down and asked myself the following clarifying questions, which I now offer to you. (You may want to grab a pen and paper for this.)

What energizes me?

What calms or soothes me?

What makes me feel accomplished at the end of the day?

What makes me (or would make me) want to get out of bed in the morning?

What activities or relationships do I *want* to make time for?

What activities or relationships do I *need* to make time for? (Be picky here. *Should do* isn't the same as *need to*.)

What activities or relationships am I making time for that don't fit either of the two criteria above? What would happen if I stopped engaging in them?

Ideally, how often would I like guilt-free downtime, rest time, and me time?

Ideally, how often would I like to spend time socializing with friends or family?

Take time now to look over your answers, then list what activities you want to keep, which ones you'd like to add, and the ones you can either delegate or let go. I call this process "stuffing the pillow."

Stuffing the Pillow (or Planner)

I like to think of my day as a pillow. When I don't have enough stuffing in my pillow, it's flat and a little sad, and I feel restless because there's nothing lifting and supporting me. But when it is too stuffed, it becomes stiff and results in exhaustion and strain. How we fill our planner is much the same. When we leave it empty, our life can feel flat and depressing. But an overstuffed planner will leave us sitting up in bed at night, stressed out, and trying to figure out how we'll ever fit everything in.

Just as each individual has their own pillow fluff preference, the perfectly stuffed planner looks different for each person (or even for different seasons of one's life). Introverts tend to need more downtime built into their schedule. Mom and I both need regular open days to meander at our own pace, but too many of those in a row and we begin feeling bored and isolated. My mother-in-law, an elementary school teacher and textbook extrovert, likes to fill almost every hour of her schedule with activities involving friends and family, but she always goes to bed early and wakes up early. Good rest, quiet mornings, and a rare Sunday off are enough downtime for her. Any more than that and she starts to get fidgety. When I compare my schedule to hers, I look like a hermit. But I know I don't function well with that level of activity. We can't compare what we accomplish with someone else who has more natural energy or capacity for socializing or is in a different stage of life than we are.

Nourished women have figured out how much stuffing leaves them satisfied and feeling a "good tired" when they lay their head down at night. In other words, they have designed a schedule that fits their personality.

"Let Me Check My Planner ..."

We've all had them, and we've all found them in May at the bottom of our purse untouched since February. After years of trying my phone, my computer, pocket-sized planners, and a big family calendar, I've come full circle back to what I used in grade school, a big spiral-bound paper planner. Picking out the perfect planner brought me right back to my favorite part of middle school—selecting the Trapper Keeper that I would carry down the school halls with pride for the next nine months. I splurged on a brightly colored customized planner from ErinCondren .com. My name and website are printed on the front, and it comes with colorful stickers (also customizable) for remembering events. Adding "Dentist Appointment" to my schedule has never been so rewarding.

The investment in the cute design of my new planner made me want to show it off, keep it out where I could see it, and created an excitement I once reserved for my beloved Trapper Keeper. For what it's worth, I say skip the professional leather-bound planner and go straight for the planner that pleases your inner twelve-year-old. Target generally has some cute modern options, and several sellers on Etsy will customize a planner to your exact needs and send you the file so you can have it printed and bound to your own liking—perfect for tech-savvy, controlling perfectionists. Of course, a legal pad can work just fine too.

Mom loses most of the expensive planners she's purchased with amazing regularity, so each day she just uses a lined notebook pad and a cheap clipboard. She plans her basic week on the top page, then orders her day on the next page. She uses the computer calendar to keep up with major events and dates because she doesn't lose her laptop as easily as she loses (or accidently washes and dries) her paper calendars. Find whatever jazzes you to get up and make a plan, which leads me to the next nourishing schedule discovery.

Establish Morning Rituals

Every morning when I worked full time for a communication-skills training company, I walked into the office kitchen and looked out the bay window overlooking a vineyard (it was quite the office view). I put a bag of green tea into my favorite insulated porcelain mug and poured water from the always-hot-and-ready water filter. Then I sat down at my desk. With one hand wrapped around the warm mug, I used the other to open up my to-do list and prioritize my day. Every day, the same soothing morning ritual.

For a season, I had to train a very chatty, bordering-on-needy woman to take over part of my job. As soon as she sat at the desk beside mine each morning, she started in with questions about my personal life, my role in the office, our filing systems, my preference for dark or milk chocolate ... basically anything that popped into her head. She asked these questions in a constant flow of interruption after interruption. As soon as I gathered a thought, she too had gathered a thought ... and she spoke all of them aloud, never thinking to keep even one to herself. I answered her questions and acknowledged her groundbreaking insights with one-word responses or head nods, hoping she'd soon get the point that I wasn't feeling up for chitchat, and that I had a job that required some focused concentration, in addition to training her for her job ... which she should have been working on.

About a week into training, she finally said frankly, "You're kind of grumpy in the mornings. You must not be a morning person."

I shrugged my shoulders, "You got me."

I promised her I'd "cheer up" and answer all her questions at nine each morning after I'd had time to settle in. I could see her over my shoulder biting her tongue. It was visibly hard for her to wait. By nine she was like a puppy let out of her crate, practically running, jumping, and licking my hand, so happy was she to finally get some attention.

What she didn't understand was this: I wasn't actually grumpy. In fact, I loved those mornings. They were almost sacred to me. Until the arrival of the Girl with No Social Filter, we had an unspoken office rule: everyone got to come in and begin their morning routines and get settled in before demands and requests started rolling in. Friendly hellos and good mornings were about all we shared as we broke in the day. This newbie was breaking the code, tinkering with my transition from home to office. I suppose *that* made me a little grumpy, but not because I am not a morning person, but because I *love* my mornings. Needless to say, she didn't last long in our office. Picking up social cues and reading people is a crucial skill for working in a communication training firm.

Even now, though I no longer work an eight-to-five job, the morning ritual of starting the coffee, warming up Jackson's oatmeal, sitting across the table from him as he eats and I sip, is one of my favorite parts of the day. It's a predictable routine: in a day that could bring thousands of unknowns, we can count on the rhythm of the morning. I rely on those ten minutes to caffeinate into a functioning human, and Jackson knows he will get a good breakfast (the same thing every day) and a little focused Mommy attention.

Creating and protecting our morning rituals is one of the most nourishing acts we can do for ourselves. Much has been written about winding down for bedtime, and the rituals of bathing, brushing our teeth, quiet reading, and kissing our loved ones good-night. But mornings are just as vital, and sadly we often let them unwind into chaos, setting a tone for the day that keeps our stomach in hurried knots. Whether it's hot tea and a Bible on the back porch or lemon-infused ice water before a morning jog or a sit-down breakfast accompanied by devotions with the whole family, it is important to find what energizes you, what makes you want to jump (or at least crawl) out of bed each morning. Making

mornings sacred ensures you'll have at least some stores of nourishment to face what the rest of the day brings.

Look at the list you made earlier. If you don't have a morning
routine already, see if you can imagine what a perfect start to your
day would look like, then capture those thoughts on paper. Let
those around you know that this will be your new morning ritual,
and ask for respect in helping you establish it. You may need to
set your alarm fifteen minutes earlier or, if you have early-rising
young children, help them establish their own morning routine or
incorporate them into yours in some way. Maybe they can color or
paint every morning or watch an educational cartoon while they
eat their breakfast. As you establish your morning routine, you can
encourage older children to start their own nourishing morning
rituals as well by getting them their own planner where they can
jot down their day's schedule or letting them play uplifting music
in the bathroom while they get ready. Let them experience how
much better it feels when we start the day off on the right foot.

The Pull

I think one of the hardest parts of being a woman is "the pull."
The pull of your children, your husband, a career, the church. The
pull to be there for our friends, to exercise and eat well, to have
hobbies, to be educated about politics and up on the latest fashion
trends. We constantly feel pulled in different directions. I think of
an octopus stretched out in a circle with eight buckets just within
reach. If she stretches, she can just barely have a tentacle in each
bucket. But she's strained and can't really experience what's *inside*
the bucket. To reach fully into a bucket, she must pull away from
the others.

Despite our efforts to be stretched out like an octopus with a
tentacle in each bucket, studies show that people actually do their
best work when focused on a single task. Even self-proclaimed

master multitaskers were proven less efficient when doing more than one thing at a time. With this in mind, I have found a lot less brain frazzle when I follow a treasured scheduling secret that my mom once shared with me.

BECKY

The $1500 Secret to Scheduling Success

Years ago I would often travel to Nashville, and when I did, I tried to stay with a delightful, gregarious couple who owned a bed and breakfast called the Rose Garden. It cost the same as a hotel, but it offered a roaring fireplace with a comfy couch, an outdoor hot tub, a little kitchen and dining table, a patio overlooking a well-tended rose garden, and best of all, the company of the two charming owners who were happy newlyweds at midlife. Like quiet elves they would bring breakfast or treats, always home-cooked, and leave them for me to enjoy by the fire or out on the patio if the weather was pretty. Over time we became friends, and on my visits they began asking me into their home for dinner or a glass of wine and a catch-up chat.

The husband was a financial planner with a head for business and a heart for his lovely wife, who kept busy growing roses and cooking gourmet meals. Their lives seemed ordered, their businesses were booming, but they also seemed so ... relaxed. Balanced. They had an active social life, loved to dance and entertain. But they also had quiet time to rest and read and trim the roses and whip up New Orleans bread pudding and mouth-watering huevos rancheros.

"Okay," I asked one evening as we sat visiting, "what's your secret for such a balanced life?"

"Do you really want to know?" he asked. "Because it will cost you fifteen hundred dollars."

"Come again?" I asked with a laugh.

"Well, that is what I paid to learn this secret at a high-dollar 'success in business' type weekend. But for you, since we're friends, I'll share it for free."

I was all ears.

"Okay," he said, handing me a piece of paper and pencil, "write this down: Work Days. Stuff Days. Off Days."

"And?"

"That's it," he said. "Plan your life by days and give each day your complete focus. Work Days are the days when you do what brings in the bulk of your income. For salesmen it's making calls. For writers it's buckling down for a marathon day of writing. People spend a lot of time putting off the actual work that brings in the most income."

I nodded in recognition. "What are Stuff Days?"

"Just what it sounds like. These are the days you get stuff done. That might mean anything from paying bills to clearing out our in-box, to doing the dry cleaning, to getting the housecleaning and laundry done. Doctor or hair appointments. You know, all that stuff we have to do that doesn't yield income but has to be done for peace of mind and order."

"Okay, I got it."

"Finally," he said, "you must absolutely schedule in Free Days, at least one per week, preferably two. These are the days when you don't think about business or work at all. Days when you *totally* disconnect and do whatever refreshes you, whether it is going out to lunch with a friend, reading a book followed by a long nap, or playing a round of golf. "

"Brilliant," I said.

And from that point on, I tried to divide my week into the three kinds of days. As a work-at-home mom, however, I modified it a bit and also tucked in some Kid Days, days when I tried to do something with my children as the main focus. (In fact, when the kids were younger, Kid Days took the place of Work Days, since my main "job" was being their mom, though I must admit the financial payoff was lousy.)

Still using this basic model years later, I plan my week on Sunday, and typically it goes something like this. Monday, Wednesday, and Thursday are Writing Days. (Meaning I spend at least four to five hours writing, blogging, or other marketing support for books.) Tuesday is usually my Stuff Day, with lots of errands: groceries, library, and so on. Fridays are Free Days. I will either enjoy a solid day alone without guilt or meet a friend for lunch. Often Greg and I will go out to dinner and a movie. Occasionally the two of us will take the whole day off together and drive around town hitting estate sales. Saturday is a Stuff Day that mostly involves laundry and deeper home cleaning. Sunday is another Free Day. We attend church, but we keep meals light and easy, and guilt-free naps are a high priority.

Put More "Whoo-Hoo!" in Your To-Dos

There is one other secret to making your schedule a lot more enjoyable, and that is to pair something you don't like to do very much with something you love. Or at the very least, promise yourself a small treat when you finish an unpleasant task. Irish-born novelist Iris Murdoch wrote that "one of the secrets to a happy life is continuous small treats."[6] Indeed. There are days I live from small treat to small treat, like an easily distracted puppy who needs a doggie treat to stay focused and on task.

Pairing up something pleasant with something unpleasant increases the fun in the dailiness of life. Think of the small tasks that you have to do but dread. I hate unloading the dishwasher and folding clothes, for example. But when I pair these things with the treat of listening to a good audiobook or watching a cooking show on TV, the task instantly becomes more enjoyable. For a long time

I looked forward to using the elliptical machine at the gym as long I could read from my Kindle while I worked out or could meet up to work out with a friend.

I will often pair writing with the delightful experience of sitting by the fireplace at our local Starbucks. Another way I get lots of writing done is on road trips with Greg. He drives while listening to an audiobook on tape (using earphones), and I type away the hours without distraction. Just being together, doing our own thing, as the world whizzes by is one of my fun zones.

If I can't think of a way to pair up something pleasant with a dreaded chore, I may simply push through and endure the task, then reward myself with a treat afterward. Sometimes I'll set a timer or turn on a song and say to myself, "Okay, Becky, give this task five minutes of your one hundred percent focused time and see what you can accomplish." And I work like mad. It's fun to see what can be done in such a short amount of time. And then I give myself a small reward, a piece of dark chocolate or five minutes to catch up on Facebook or to peruse Pinterest. The bigger the chore, the bigger the reward. Perhaps thirty minutes for a guilt-free nap or curling up with a good book. If I finish a big deadline, well, that means I will arrange a celebratory lunch with my girlfriends. I also love unfettered time to explore books at the library or our local indie bookstore, Tattered Cover. Maybe I'll spend twenty dollars on a new fun shirt from Ross or TJ Maxx. Or browse our local thrift store for a three-dollar find. Or download a new Kindle book I've been wanting.

As you plan your week, you may want to put a star by the chores you normally dread. Then go back and see if you can pair them up with an enjoyable activity to increase the fun factor; or think of a treat you can give yourself when the task is done and put this in parentheses beside the task. Having something small to look forward to makes a big difference.

Life is too short not to make it as much fun as possible. By scheduling lots of small pleasures into your days, you squeeze a lot more joy into your time on earth.

RACHEL

Like Mom, I too have found that having days or large blocks of time for certain tasks makes me more efficient. Because my schedule as a mom is less flexible, I usually organize my time into blocks rather than full days. My day naturally gets divided into segments of before Jackson's nap, during his nap, and after his nap. I might run errands in the morning, write during nap time, and leave the afternoon for some time focused on Jackson. And then I have two days a week where he goes to school from 9:00 to 2:00. Those days are for writing. I pull out my writing schedule and forget all the other to-do lists.

I try to have one home-improvement day a week. Between offering snacks and playing Legos, I do laundry and general house cleaning. Then during Jackson's nap, I "take off" work and do some sort of bigger home-improvement project, like cleaning out a closet, making a crafty decoration for the house, or working in the garden. Because organizing is truly fun and relaxing for me, I sometimes consider this my "Off Day." My personality type thrives in a clean, organized home, so time to do this is more nourishing than, say, a day at the spa or browsing the mall.

One of my favorite things about being a mom is that making time for play is a natural priority. I often free my afternoons to simply enter Jackson's small imaginative world with my whole heart. We may plan or happen upon a fun activity. For example, I taught him last week how to boogie like a Beach Boy to the song "Barbara Ann." Later that evening while cooking dinner, he walked in the kitchen humming and reached out his hand to me and belted out, "Come take my hand." Jackson is a people person to the max, so I may arrange a playdate with a friend I enjoy who has a child my son loves to play with. He gets me out of my hermit shell. Then there are the times when I follow Jackson's whims, whether that means walking to the park, making mud pies in the sandbox, or playing hide-and-seek. These blocks are totally for Jackson, to really pour into him, so he's filled up with love when I have to schedule a Work Day away from him.

And of course, my husband gets blocked in regularly on my planner with a night out or a hot date on the couch in our pj's. After all, the hope is that your spouse will always be your best soul mate and playmate.

So now, when I experience the often overwhelming and simultaneous pulls of life, I sit down with my pretty planner and organize blocks of time to go with my top priorities. I schedule blocks of time for must-do priorities, plus blocks of time that simply fill me up, energize, and nourish me. Besides work and chores, I pencil in time for exercise, friendship, cooking, prayer, reading, and visiting family. And then I look back and make sure my agenda won't send me slipping and sliding in the mud as I race from one thing to the next.

Whether you schedule your time in complete days or blocks of time or work through an organized task list each day, find a method that helps *you* design the life that nourishes you the most. In fact, before you move on to the next section, you may want to look once more at your lists from the beginning of the chapter and, applying any concepts that struck a chord with you here, plan out the week ahead of you.

PART 3

Nourished Bodies, Nourished Selves

Chapter 7

At Home in Our Own Skin

Nourishing Self-Acceptance

There is nothing more rare, nor more beautiful,
than a woman being unapologetically herself;
comfortable in her perfect imperfection.
To me, that is the true essence of beauty.
Steve Maraboli

BECKY

There are so many areas of myself—my body, my face, my personality bent, my limitations, my unique needs and wants—that have taken me years to accept and embrace.

Last night I told my husband, "One of the joys of living on the side of life where you are closer to your death than your birth is that issues I've struggled with since puberty—petty jealousies, desire for significance, spending way more time worrying about my appearance than my inner beauty—are finally, finally beginning to fade in light of what matters most. It's a surprising relief to feel more at home inside this body that houses the real me, the me that will never die: my soul."

He smiled and nodded in agreement. I honestly do not know

of a human being more comfortable in his own skin than my husband. He does not let his gray hair (what's left of it) or a few extra pounds hold him back from feeling at ease and confident in the boardroom or bedroom. "I just am what I ams," he'll say, as he smiles and takes me into his arms with such natural ease and confidence. Greg has taught me more about self-acceptance by sheer example than I've ever learned from mentors, therapists, or self-help books.

"I want you to know something, Becky," Greg said, a few minutes after I admitted my long struggle to make peace with the loss of youthful beauty. "To me you can never be anything but beautiful. Even when you are a hundred years old, I will look in your eyes and see the alluring woman I fell in love with."

If beauty is in the eye of the beholder, I've married a man with an A-plus Beholder. There is nothing so beautifying as loving someone and being loved in return. Even with my husband's capacity to see only the beauty in me, however, it has been a great struggle to come to the place where I am truly at home in my own skin.

Some days I think, "Whew! I've finally arrived at the point of total body acceptance!" And to be fair to myself, I have come a long way.

Until.

Lord help me ...

I see an unflattering photo of myself.

Especially on Facebook.

No kidding, a picture of myself at an unflattering angle can send me into the Slough of Despond, the pit of self-loathing for days. And if someone posts that picture on Facebook ... let me just say that I'm pretty certain I hold the world speed record for untagging ugly photos. I know I'm not alone in this. Most women feel less than delighted when they spy unflattering photos of themselves on social media. But then I discovered that my harsh criticism of photos of myself had a hurtful impact on someone I adore. My daughter.

And that's when I knew, I had some more self-acceptance to do. Not only for my sake, but for hers.

Last spring, Rachel and I had a photography session at my house together, because we needed some professional headshots to go with our first book and blog. It was a fun day. Our photographer, Molly, was talented and friendly and helped us relax, but my initial reactions to the results were … well, I think I'll let Rachel take over and tell the rest of this story from her point of view.

RACHEL

"How about this one?" I asked mom, holding up a flowy coral blouse. I glanced out of her upstairs bedroom window overlooking her backyard. The sun was shining, I could see a few blades of grass, and red tips of tulips were peeking up, as if on tiptoe, from the fresh blanket of snow—a Colorado "spring surprise."

"Oh, that will look perfect with this top I wanted to wear," Mom answered, walking into her closet. We coordinated outfits to earrings and laid the finished "looks" on her king-sized bed. Once wardrobe decisions had been made, I took over half of her vanity. Side by side, we did our hair. She curled hers with an iron; I tamed my natural curls with defrizzer. I brushed on my new powdered foundation, bought especially for this occasion. (After all, it is not every day a girl gets publicity pictures taken for her first book.) I had worn it once in Texas with no issue, but my first attempt in dry Colorado did not go well. My skin looked as if it were flaking off. Panic set in. *Why didn't I just pack the cheap familiar makeup I'd been using for years?*

With me near tears and minutes from the photographer's arrival, my mom quickly jumped in, handing me her makeup remover and helping to wash off my shedding face. She rubbed a little of her face lotion on my cheeks and blew on it to help it dry quicker. Then she dabbed the wide, angled brush into my powder and gently tapped off the excess. As she worked her magic, sweeping the powder across my cheeks, I had a close view of my mother, all made-up. I admired her olive skin. She had a bronze glow to her, as she always does. You'd never guess she'd just been through a long, cold Colorado winter.

The doorbell rang. It was the photographer. Mom handed me the brush with a last few instructions and an affirming, "You are stunning."

I nervously carried on, finishing up my makeup as fast as I could. I could hear Mom's voice downstairs showing the photographer around. They were laughing like old friends already. No surprise there. Mom has a way of making people feel at ease around her, like you've known her all your life. She's been that way as long as I can remember.

I used to travel with her on occasion, watch her entertain crowds of laughing women, and then help at her book table. After her speech, women would line up for the chance to tell her their funny "Becky Story"—the term fans and friends have coined for occasions when they do something unbelievably ditzy or forgetful, the sort of embarrassing moments you just have to tell a friend about so you can laugh together; otherwise, you just might cry. We all have these moments, but my mom has them more than anyone I know. Just as often, however, the woman in line for "a book and a hug and a chat" might share something deep, a story they trusted Mom to hear with understanding and grace. I've stood awkwardly, fiddling my thumbs, hungry and bored, more times than I can count, watching a woman open up to her, tell her things they couldn't tell anyone else. Undoubtedly, a sweet lady would see me standing there waiting and would come chat with me. "You look just like your mother," they would dote, "just lovely. You must be so proud of your mom." That was the opening line.

Every time. I was a teenager with an appetite for food beyond the typical finger sandwiches served at ladies' luncheonettes. I was also eager to go explore a new city with my mom. So the long wait by her side at the book table wasn't my favorite part of these events. But I appreciated the women who saw me in the room and made me feel at ease. And yes, I was proud of my mom. Very proud.

But I digress. I finally got my makeup done, then wandered downstairs where I found my mom and the photographer near our first "props"—a set of turquoise coffee cups. We got right to it, taking picture after picture in several settings from Mom's dining-room table, to the kitchen, and finally out into the backyard where the sun shone at a perfect angle in one green patch where the snow had melted.

A few days later, after I'd flown back to Texas, we got the proofs online, about a hundred pictures. I flipped through them and narrowed the ones I liked down to my top three-to-four favorite poses in each setting—about twenty-five total—and sent the list to my mom. I expected that she would be quite picky. She's never liked seeing pictures of herself. Photos are a trigger that sends her back to a painful time in her life. I know this; I expected this wouldn't be easy for her.

But when she sent me a list back with every reason she hated almost every single photo of herself, I just sat at my computer and cried. I wasn't concerned she'd narrowed down the selection of usable pictures. We really needed only one or two headshots for the publisher. What I did care about was that there was a bully saying terrible, mean, false things about my mama, and I wanted to yell at that bully. I wanted to tell her to shut up and quit whispering lies into my mother's heart. I wanted to tell her, "I look just like my mother!" and that I was insulted that she didn't like my mom's nose—because it's my nose—or her squinty-eyed, buck-toothed laugh—because that's *my* laugh too.

Instead, I simply wrote back and told Mom that I wished she was seeing the same pictures of herself that I was. Because what I saw was absolutely lovely.

What is a grown daughter to do?

Love her. Support her. Send her pictures for approval before I share them on Facebook. Save my favorite photos of her—those moments of her laughing or kneeling down with her grandsons—for my own personal albums. The pictures she hates, but I love. The pictures that capture real moments, not perfect ones. Because it's important to her, I do try really hard to take her picture at the most flattering angles. That's all I really know to do.

And then I vow to never let some negative voice tell me I'm not beautiful. In front of my children I will speak of my beauty with confidence. I will teach my son to see all women as beautiful. "Look how pretty Mommy looks," I tell him as we look in the mirror, first thing in the morning before I've even smoothed out my frizzy ponytail. And I will point out my mom's beauty. "Look at Nonny! Doesn't she look beautiful?" I can't change the way my mom sees herself. But I refuse to believe that my nose is too pointy or my eyes too squinty. They are my mother's nose and my mother's eyes. They are beautiful.

The ironic thing is, I think my mom is the reason I have never questioned my beauty or really put a lot of importance on it. She's always told me with such conviction how pretty I am. I just never questioned that she was wrong. And trust me, I've had some awkward years, taken a lot of terrible photos, and experienced some hurtful rejection based on my appearance. I've also been told all my life that I look just like my mama ... and it never occurred to me this wasn't a compliment.

Long before I discovered hair gel (that lesson could have come a few years earlier, Mom) and makeup, my mom was teaching me to look past appearances and see my peers as children of God, as I was. In first grade, when she discovered one little boy in our class couldn't afford ice cream on Fridays, she paid for his for the rest of the school year so he'd be included. She never let me speak unkindly of classmates. In fact, if she sensed my group of friends was leaving a girl out, she'd arrange a sleepover for me and her. It was serious business. In our family, we did not dismiss, categorize, or hurt people based on their appearance or quirks — we always looked at their heart. I'm often around women who, by typical standards, are more beautiful than I am, but it rarely bothers me. Because of these valuable childhood lessons, I just don't feel that how beautiful you are or what size you are matters all that much.

I don't share this to shame my mom or other women who struggle with feeling unattractive. We all have our battles, and because of some critical voices from my mother's past, she's struggled hard and long to believe she is lovely, as is. I'm grateful that she has helped me see myself differently than she sees herself. But I admit, the older I get and the more I look like the woman she puts down, the more I start to question whether my beauty is something tethered to my youth ... or tethered to my soul.

I just wish she could see what I see. I wish she could fire the bully in her brain and replace it with my thoughts of her, or Greg's view of her, or better yet, God's view of His wonderful creation: my warm, witty, beautiful mother.

BECKY

This is the second time I've read Rachel's honest, impassioned words, and both times I have wept afterward. Because it took a lot of courage to speak her truth. And because everything she wrote is exactly right.

And because I love her so much, I've determined to find a way to love myself too. Just as I am. To embrace the real me as I'm caught in a snapshot, enjoying my grandkids and others, from any camera point of view. Because it isn't the camera's point of view that matters the most. It is the point of view of those who love me, who see me through the eyes of A-plus beholders.

And so, for the past year, I've determined to become an A-plus beholder of me, myself, and I. Here are a few ideas that have really helped the process along.

Research Beauty in Your Body Type

For an instant pick-me-up, Google your body type and then add the words "beautiful" and "fashion," and you will see a gorgeous array of women who look like you, decked out in styles that bring out their va-va-voom. You can even make a Pinterest page called "Beautiful Women with My Body Type" and start pinning away. You'll find dozens of ideas for clothing, shoes, accessories, and more that spark creativity and make you want to dive into your closet for new, flattering, and fun ways to wear old clothes.

My body type (and my beautiful daughter's too) is curvy on top and bottom, and at five-foot-two we are decidedly short. So we look best in fashions you see on curvy gals like Nigella Lawson, Oprah Winfrey, or Kim Kardashian (when she wears clothes that are bigger than a napkin). I never met a three-quarter-length-sleeve jersey knit shirt or dress, with a wide boat or sweetheart neckline, that I didn't adore. I love skirts that flair and swish, and I like them a little on the long side.

I loved the show *What Not to Wear* and was actually relieved to discover that although our body type can be dressed to look fashionable and savvy, it was one of Clinton and Stacy's biggest challenges. Pants that fit our hips are too large at the waist. Shirts that hug our waists won't button across our boobs. So they have to do lots of tailoring to make most on-the-rack fashions work for this body type. No wonder clothes shopping is no picnic for either of us!

I know, even as I write this, that not being able to find clothes that flatter and fit is unquestionably a First World problem, but who is to say that I may not be better equipped (or at least dressed for) helping to solve Third World problems if I could find a pair of jeans and button-up work shirt that actually fit?

Make Peace with Your Jiggly Bits

One of my lifelong struggles has been to make peace with my thighs. I remember how relieved I was to read that Anne Lamott, one of my favorite writers, also struggled with this, and I'm sure we aren't alone. In a classic article for *Salon* magazine, "A Day at the Beach with My 'Aunties,'" Anne determines to employ Loving Acceptance toward her own jiggly, aging body, and creatively names her thighs "the aunties." She "decided to treat them as if they were beloved elderly aunties, who did embarrassing things like roll their stockings into tubes around their ankles at the beach," but who she was proud of anyway, "because they were so great in every important way."[7]

Anne's words helped me, too, to begin to see my flawed body in more compassionate ways. I realized that I could change the way I looked at my thighs and see them through more benevolent eyes. It was a start.

No matter what cute names I called them, however, there came a day when I knew, for me, it was time for me to stop letting the aunties waddle around wearing shorts in public. I was fifty, and my thighs had served me well, but they looked like they had severe hail damage and it was time to just let go in a way that brought me a lot more peace. The choice wasn't made with anger or disgust. It was freeing, actually, to just give all my shorts away. As a gift to celebrate "The End of the Era of Shorts-Wearing," I bought some comfortable cute cropped pants and cool, cotton, flowy bohemian skirts along with a couple of swim skirts for the pool. I've accepted that my thighs and I are happier with more swaddling, but this doesn't mean I stopped exercising them and feeding them healthy foods or have totally given up the battle of their "cute little bulges." It just means that while I'm working on whittling them down a bit, I'm not loathing or hating them, yelling at them, or calling them bad names ... and I'm not letting them hold me back from enjoying all the perks of spring and summer and feeling pretty in my own skin. My thighs and I are at a nice serene place right now. We met in the middle and found our happy place. I made nourishing changes to my thoughts *and* my wardrobe, and I'm happier for having done both.

P.S.: May I just add my thanks to JLo, Beyonce, Kim Kardashian, and Christina Hendricks for doing their part to help us ladies with a little more junk in our trunk feel like we got sexier almost overnight, along with your rising popularity—without us having to expend any effort at all. What a gift. We, and our backsides, thank you.

RACHEL

Say Goodbye to "When I ..."

How many things are you putting on hold, until you either return to some idealized former self or become an idealized future self? Do you ever say to yourself (as I have), things like ...

When I ... get a firm stomach, I'll plan a beach vacation.

When I ... get rid of this cellulite, I'll let my husband see me naked.

When I ... lose the baby weight, I'll buy new clothes.

When I ... get my teeth whitened and hair done and my kitchen perfect, I'll record YouTube cooking demos.

Last spring, I kept seeing the most adorable girls wearing hot-pink skinny jeans, paired with loose tops and ballet slippers or high heels. I wanted so badly to own a pair, but skinny jeans don't fit over my "python thighs" (as one of my brothers once lovingly called them) or my "huge calves," as one ex-boyfriend called them. (Gee, how did that relationship not work out?) In their defense, both guys truly, and ignorantly, thought they were dishing out compliments. Turns out these men envied "huge calves" and "python thighs," and one of them told me, "Seriously. Some dudes even pay to have calf implants." If only I could donate mine to their cause.

Anyway, back to the pants. I wasn't at my ideal size and felt sure pink skinny jeans would only accentuate my heftier-than-I'd-prefer hips. So I told myself, "If I lose ten pounds, I'll look for a pair of pink pants."

A few weeks later, without a downward budge in my weight, I stumbled across a pair of straight-leg, cropped, hot-pink pants at Kohls. Though I hadn't lost a pound, I mustered the confidence to try them on anyway. They fit over my thighs and hugged my calves just right. And I loved them. If I do say so myself, I looked every bit as adorable as the thinner girls I'd been admiring. My curves did pop in the pink, and ... what do you know? I liked it! I felt sexy and flirty and stylish. There in the dressing room I had my own hot-pink pants party, celebrating my body as it was, in that moment.

When we deprive ourselves of joy or self-acceptance until we're thinner, tanner, more muscular, better, we are telling ourselves for that whole "in-between process" we are lacking in some way ... that we are not good enough.

Goals are great, but they are meant to encourage us, not put our lives on hold.

You want some pink pants? Go get 'em, girl! The skinny girls don't have exclusive rights to fun fashion.

BECKY

If You've Got It, Put a Bow on It (If You Don't, Drape It in Black)

Midlife women like me have to seek the tricky balance between total acceptance of aging faces or sagging bodies and the desire to do everything we can to dress them up and show them off in the best possible light.

As a Southern girl, my fashion rule is this: put something big, bright — even approaching gaudy — on your best features; then put black on your body spots that you'd prefer others skim over with less notice. This is why I buy huge bright-colored earrings, scarves, and tops, and wear a lot of black on my bottom half. It's my way of saying, "Focus on the face, darlin' . . . ignore those auntie hips behind the dark curtain."

All God's Girls Are Gorgeous

I had a fascinating experience yesterday. I went to a big bridal shop with my soon-to-be daughter-in-law, Aleks, and five of her six bridesmaids. Aleks, a natural-blond beauty, had already chosen her gown, so the goal today was for the bridesmaids to find dresses (in the same color), in whatever style suited them. I had so much fun watching these gorgeous girls, who wore sizes from size 2 to 20, in every sort of body shape — all try on the same style of dress.

This is what blew me away: they'd walk out of their dressing rooms, each wearing the same style, and a few of them would look as though the dress had been made for them. Show stopping. The dress did all the right things to bring out the beauty in their figures. While the very same dress did absolutely nothing for others. It didn't matter one bit what size or shape the girl was, out of the six styles they all tried on, each of them found at least two styles that looked stunning on them, and each of them tried on dresses that caused a chorus of, "No, that's just not doin' it for you."

I was sitting in a spot where I could also watch bride after bride try on wedding gowns until the magic moment when they walked out in the "right dress," and it was as if everyone in the store knew it. In fact, one of the staff members would ring a bell to celebrate the moment.

One very young bride, who I'm guessing wore about a size 26, came out of the dressing room in a gorgeous white dress that looked as if she'd been wrapped in delicate folds of cream. A red sash at the empire waistline was the perfect touch. Everything about this dress flattered her best assets. By this time, I'd been in the bridal store for two hours and found myself totally swept away in the fun of cheering on the right dress. I found myself saying to this young woman, whom I had never met, in front of everyone: "Honey, you do not need to try on another dress. That's the *one*." The young bride looked at me, then turned toward her mother, who nodded, tears in her eyes, and said, "Yes. That's it."

I then started to get *verklempt* and tearful. Catching myself, I explained, "I'm sorry for speaking so boldly. It's just that I've been here awhile, and I keep getting all caught up in everyone's excitement. I'm starting to act like the bridal version of a Walmart greeter. Don't you think it would be a fun job to just sit here and tell brides how beautiful they are all day?"

The young woman laughed and said, "I work at Walmart! It must be a sign. High five!" And so I high-fived the bride. And when I returned to my seat, I saw once again, so clearly, that all of God's girls—in every shape and size, tall, short, thin, curvy—are indeed absolutely gorgeous.

We just need to recognize it. For the love of ourselves, our daughters, and our granddaughters.

Chapter 8

Joyful Eating

Nourishing Menus and Happy Memories

I found that if I was eating well,
there was a good chance that I was living well, too.
I found that when I prioritized dinner,
a lot of other things seemed to fall into place ...
and perhaps most important, the simple act of carving
out the ritual—a delicious homemade meal—
gave every day purpose and meaning,
no matter what else was going on in our lives.
Jenny Rosenstrach, *Dinner: A Love Story*

RACHEL

Jackson has an incredible obsession with all things related to lawn equipment. It began as soon as he could pull himself up as a baby and watch his daddy mow the lawn with the kind of rapt, almost worshipful adoration Catholics save for the pope.

At age two and a half, when other kids are watching cartoons, he begs to watch YouTube videos of men mowing the lawn or repairing a Weed Eater's carburetor or reviewing hot trends in leaf blowers. His toy lawn mower is his prized possession—in fact, he's collected three of them now; so he's never more than twenty feet from one should the urge suddenly arise to mow the carpet, tile, or dead grass.

If he's not close to an actual toy lawn mower, he will improvise. I've seen him turn his old baby bouncy chair upside down, and make expert motor noises while gliding it across the floor like a push mower. You'd be surprised how many things can double as a Weed Eater. On her last visit here, Mom gladly gave him her electric toothbrush to keep after she found carpet fibers in it. She discovered he'd been "edging" the carpet around the baseboards in the guest room.

In a pinch, he's even grabbed my leg to trim some imaginary weeds nearby.

I've tried to share his enthusiasm for mowers and Weed Eaters and edgers, I really have. But he senses the truth: I simply can't drum up the same passion he feels for lawn tools. Thankfully, however, we've found common ground in the kitchen.

Today I propped him up on his kitchen stool, then handed him a pile of cauliflower and a blunt knife while I made a curried cauliflower hash at the stove top. I turned around to check on him when I heard him making impressive "ZzzzoojZzzoooj" sounds. He paused from his "hard work" and grinned. "See my chain saw?" he asked with manly pride. Then he returned back to sawing his mound of cauliflower "woodchips."

I'm delighted he found a way to bring a "Tim the Tool Man" version of a sous-chef into our culinary experiences, delighted that our two worlds — my love for cooking and his for power tools — have made friends in the kitchen.

Though Jackson now adds his own special turbo touch to the process, cooking together has always been kind of "our thing." A friend asked him recently if he had a dog, and Jackson told her matter-of-factly, "No, I have a mommy. And she cooks with me." Well, there you have it. Who needs a dog to play with, when you have a mom to cook with?

Food Memories

Mom and I wrote our first food blog post when Jackson was just eight months old, while she was visiting my home in Texas. We were cooking Roasted Poblano Corn Chowder, and I'd given her one task while I went to rock Jackson to sleep: "Keep a sharp eye on the croutons in the oven so they don't burn, okay? Please pay attention, Mom, because I know how distracted you can get, and those are my last pieces of bread in there. We need the garnish for the pictures."

Ten minutes later I heard the searing sound of an alarm. I entered a kitchen now billowing with smoke. My mother was sheepishly fanning at a pan of hopelessly charred croutons, apologizing profusely. And thus, our career as "professional" food bloggers began — followed by writing a humorous food memoir together, based on stories, recipes, and meals we've known and loved. (And occasionally, the meals Mom burned before we got a chance to know or love them.)

After two years of sharing recipes and stories from my kitchen, my husband has learned to ask, "Have you taken a picture of my dinner plate yet, or can I eat it now?" The other day I picked up my smartphone and saw a picture Jackson had apparently taken, all on his own, of his own toddler lunch: a half-eaten peanut-butter sandwich, a neat row of teeth marks in the bread, artfully turned toward the camera. All aesthetically arranged on a blue plastic plate. I was awash with pride. He has fully embraced our family dinner routine: serve the food, snap a picture of it, pray, then eat.

I recognize now that our food blog has been much more than a log of meals and menus. The posts, recipes, and pictures also tell the history of Jackson's growing love of all things food related while working beside me in the kitchen.

In our book *We Laugh, We Cry, We Cook*, Mom wrote, "Unlike anything else, food sears itself into our memories. This is why, when we feed others, we nourish them in a myriad of surprising and memorable ways. You never know what gooey grilled-cheese sandwich or steaming bowl of basil-tomato soup will become a comforting memory forever sealed in the heart of someone you love."[8]

God creatively designed our brains to associate smells and tastes with memories, so that an aroma wafting from a restaurant's kitchen or cooking a family recipe can immediately take you back in time, to warm childhood memories.

A few months ago, Jackson and I flew for a visit to Colorado, and before I left, I made a big pot of vegan lentil soup. Mom took one bite of it and smiled. Her eyes had a faraway look. "Mmmmm, this is so good and comforting. There's something in this soup that tastes exactly like a dish my Nonny would have made. One spoonful of this soup, and I'm back in her yellow kitchen, surrounded by the aroma of something simmering on the stove and my grandmother's comforting presence."

We never figured out exactly what was in my lentil soup that took Mom immediately back to happy scenes from her girlhood, but we marveled again at the powerful ties between food and memory.

I Love It When a Plan Comes Together

I've grown increasingly aware that cooking and mealtimes are one of the best ways to build good family memories, but for a long time I never bothered with making a weekly menu plan. This isn't because I don't like planning ahead, because I am *all* about scheduling. As you already know, I salivate at the sight of a good organizer.

The reason I didn't plan menus was because, as newlyweds, Jared and I enjoyed the fun of deciding what we wanted to do for dinner together according to what we happened to be in the mood for as our work days ended. We might decide to eat out at a favorite bistro or seaside café (we lived near Galveston some of this time), or one of us would stop by the market and grab fresh ingredients, and I could take my time putting a healthy meal together. I didn't really need a plan and actually enjoyed going with the whim of the moment.

But that was then. This is now. And now my life contains an active little boy and a writing career that has grown even busier. I've learned that the busier our lives get, the more we need nourishing meals, and the more I've had to plan ahead to make them happen.

The Joy of Cooking? Feels More like the Burden of Cooking

Recently, I was speaking to a group of ladies about cooking healthy foods for our families, and sharing some of the recipes and stories from *We Laugh, We Cry, We Cook*. A woman, probably in her early fifties, came up after my speech to try my samples, and we began chatting about her desire to eat healthier. Her children were grown and out of the house; she worked full-time and was clearly, and understandably, a little tired of the daily grind. She asked, "How am I supposed to find time to cook when I don't even get home until six or seven most nights?"

But before I could answer with encouragement and tips, she interrupted, "Well, you obviously don't work, right? 'Cause if I didn't have to work, I'd be able to eat healthy too."

She *obviously* seemed to have missed the fact that I was actually "working" in that very moment — that speaking and writing were in fact real "jobs" that I manage while juggling the roles of busy coach's wife and mom of an active two-year-old. I did my best to answer her politely but couldn't help but think, *Don't most people work for the majority of their lives? Are we all supposed to put healthy eating on hold until retirement?* She went on to add, "Besides, I can't afford to eat all that healthy stuff."

Most families I know are short on either money or time, if not both. Ours is no different. I empathize. But I have found that with some planning and creativity you can avoid eating junk on the run. For example, the Simple Lentil Soup that my mom loved so much (recipe on our blog[9]) costs less than a fast-food burger, feeds a family of six, and takes thirty minutes, start to finish.

When life gets busy, it is easy for nourishing meals to go by the wayside. A new job or big project comes up, and suddenly we are eating fast food, pouring massive amounts of coffee or soda down our gullets in order to get by on less sleep, and suffering stomach pains as a consequence. The funny thing is, we would never dream of letting a child live this way. I've spent a significant amount of time and energy in the last two and a half years focusing on my son's food intake and outtake. As the saying goes, "Babies eat, poop, and sleep." Before they can learn to do anything else, these basic needs must be taken care of. In fact, ignoring them would be grounds for charges of child neglect and abuse. Not nourishing a baby? Unthinkable.

Do we think that when we grow up and life gets stressful and packed with activity that our need for healthy foods, good digestion, and a full night's sleep go away?

As I mentioned before, the crazier life gets and the older I get, the more I realize I need to concentrate on the care and feeding of ... me. As much as I love to cook and to eat, there are seasons when I don't have a lot of spare time for either. But here's what I'm learning: if I don't prioritize nourishing myself and my family, we are all gonna pay in some way. Headaches, crankiness, lack of energy, brain fog, and that awful feeling you get when you look up and realize it's time for dinner and you've got ... um ... nothing. Been there, regretted that.

It takes a lot less time and energy to plan ahead—creating

menus that are quick and easy, yummy and healthy—than it does to scrounge the fridge and pantry in a panic, trying to throw together something edible at the last minute. In fact, the heavier the work deadlines, the more I need to plan. Even if that plan includes a couple of take-out meals or heating up leftovers.

Also, when I make eating well and meal planning a priority, everything else in our lives seems to fall into place more easily. For example, I'm writing this chapter during "book deadline week," when every spare minute is needed to write and edit. Last week I made a batch of spinach-and-mushroom empanadas and froze them. Then I rinsed, dried, and chopped a big bunch of kale for salads. Because I was "kind to my future self," it took me only about ten minutes to get a healthy dinner on the table tonight.

Since food is the stuff that fuels our life, when we make healthy menus a priority, we make ourselves and our family a priority. When we choose a more calming and intentional approach to cooking and serving meals, we are upping the chance for creating positive food memories that will enrich our lives and our kids' lives for years to come.

Tips for Planning Nourishing Meals

1. Organize your recipes

I love Pinterest! There, I said it. I don't spend a lot of time browsing on Pinterest, but when I come across a recipe that looks easy, healthy, and delicious, I simply add it to my *Recipes I'd Like to Try* board. Once I try it, if it's a winner, it goes straight to the *Recipes I Love* board. If not, I can delete it or make myself a note, "Too much heat for Jackson. Try again with less spice." When I sit down to plan a menu, I open up these two Pinterest boards with their bright pictures and quick descriptions and pull together a menu. (Many of the "Recipes I Love" come from our food blog at www.welaughwecrywecook.com, since we tend to only blog about our tried-and-true go-to recipes.) Then I jot down the ingredients I need for the recipes on my grocery list.

Of course, you can do something similar with paper folders to collect clippings or computer files with Word documents or pdfs for each recipe you find online. Be sure to tuck in a page with all your favorite recipes from cookbooks (include page numbers) so you can quickly locate them when needed.

2. Go with what you know and have on hand

Because I think cooking should be a mix of comfort and adventure, of the familiar and a little risk, I try only one or maybe two new recipes a week. On a high stress week, I'm likely to go straight to the *Recipes I Love* file to keep things simple and predictable.

To stretch the groceries and your budget, do a quick check of the pantry, freezer, and fridge before making menus to see if there is anything you need to use up that you already have on hand, and try to work those ingredients into the next week's meals. If you're stumped, type a few ingredients you need to use up in your search engine along with the word "recipe" to find new ways to use old faves. One of our favorite meals to use up bits and pieces of leftovers is Mom's easy Rustic Iron Skillet Pot Pie recipe (also on our blog).[10]

3. Keep it simple, sweetheart

As far as menus and grocery lists go, I've tried lots of approaches over the years, from online services to phone apps to customized documents organized by my grocery store's aisles. All have worked for different seasons, but for now, I've come back to a simple notebook dedicated to menu planning. I write the week's menu on one page and the grocery list on the next. And like many people, I keep a little notepad by my refrigerator to jot down basics that need replenishing while I'm cooking. Simple and effective. Of course, if you like using customized spreadsheets or find the apps that generate grocery lists to be timesaving, then go for it. Whatever you do, just keep it simple for you, so you don't dread the task.

Even though "organization" is not my mom's natural gift, the one area where she consistently plans ahead is for the week's menus. "It's probably because I enjoy it so much," she tells me. "After all, it's a guilt-free thirty minutes that I can sit and think about food."

After planning the week's menus on a legal pad, Mom posts them on a dry-erase board on the fridge so it is always there at a glance to remind her of what to thaw or prep earlier in the day. A dry-erase board provides a flexible way to mix and match meals or make last-minute changes when reality and preferences hit your well-laid plans. If friends ask you over for an impromptu dinner on Tuesday, you can just postpone Tuesday's meal to Saturday with a quick erase and rewrite. If you don't feel like salmon on Monday, switch it out with Wednesday's quesadillas. This way you can stay "organized" but flexible.

4. Decide on a healthy eating approach that works for you

My family has followed a mostly plant-based diet for almost four years. It works for us. It gives me clear boundaries for meal planning, which I find comforting. Since we eat a lot of produce, I can't afford to eat all organic, so I've decided to use the Environmental Working Group's Dirty Dozen to help guide my organic produce purchases.[11] If it's on the Dirty Dozen, meaning it's been shown to have the highest amount of pesticides among all fruits and vegetables, then I only buy organic. I also only buy organic soy and corn because most conventional soy and corn is genetically modified, something I try to avoid when possible. When making my grocery lists, I always mark the items that I need to buy organic. Those are my personal clear boundaries. I like clear boundaries.

Mom, on the other hand, is a flexitarian. She eats a mostly

vegetarian diet, occasionally eats vegan, and occasionally has some meat or fish. She always chooses real whole foods over processed or low fat / sugar-free versions. She embraces the idea of listening to her body and giving it what it's asking for in the moment, even if only a few bites.

I find moderation to be more mental work than I want to deal with. For example, I absolutely cannot be trusted with a pan of brownies. I know this about myself. I cannot only have one. Not possible. Ain't happening. So I simply don't make or buy sweets unless I'm entertaining. It's another one of my boundaries. I like my boundaries. I *need* my boundaries.

Having a few clear parameters around your menu makes planning healthy meals easier. (And keeps you from impulsively buying a dozen donuts and a bag of chocolate chips because they are on sale.)

5. Schedule time to meal plan and grocery shop

There will always be something that seems more important than meal planning or going to the store. But healthy meals don't "just happen" without some planning, especially when you are changing your eating habits, and everything takes just a little longer until you get past the learning curve. Put meal planning and grocery shopping on your planner every week or at least on a regular schedule that works for you. A friend of mine who works full time plans a menu for the whole month and then buys groceries once a week. Knowing the menu weeks in advance allows her coupon-savvy husband to shop for the best deals all month long. Yes, her husband is the couponer.

Which brings me to another tip: don't be afraid to outsource grocery shopping. Eating is a family affair, and menu planning and grocery shopping can be too. I enjoy meal planning and cooking, but grocery shopping is not my favorite chore. Jared, on the other hand, will actually volunteer to take Jackson and go grocery shopping. And get this … he kind of *enjoys* it. He even has the patience to let Jackson push his own miniature cart or walk beside him instead of riding in the buggy. I believe my husband's spiritual gift is patience, and to help "fan into flame" this gift from God, I give him regular opportunities to practice it in the aisles of the grocery store with our two-year-old son.

6. Freeze your frenzy away

Freezer meals have become something of a trend in the food world, and for a reason — they are amazing. Having a homemade dinner all prepped and cooked ahead of time, just waiting to be defrosted, warmed, or baked is one of the absolute kindest things you can do for yourself (or a friend). I try to plan one meal a week that can be doubled and frozen. Things like veggie burgers, soups, refried beans, even pizza can easily be doubled and frozen. While you're making dough and chopping up pizza toppings, make an extra for the freezer; instead of making two quarts of soup, make four. Between leftovers and freezer meals, you can easily get to the point where you are only really cooking dinner three times a week. The rest is just filling in side dishes and quickly "repackaging" yesterday's tacos into today's Mexican salad.

Breakfast foods like muffins, waffles, pancakes, and oatmeal freeze fabulously. Make one big weekend breakfast and then have your morning meals ready for the whole week. Desserts like cookies and bars and cupcakes are also great freezer foods. I keep individual portions of healthier treats in the freezer. When a class party comes up, all I have to do is pop a vegan cupcake into my son's bag, and he's ready to party with the rest of them. And when I really want something sweet, I can pull out one treat for myself. It's a lot easier not to overeat a whole batch of brownies if you immediately wrap them into individual servings and put them in the freezer. I'm telling you, ladies, freeze that frenzy away!

7. Make a list of quick-'n'-easy meals

We all have days when we're exhausted, sick, or behind schedule. On these days you want to have a list of no-brainer dinners that you can pull together in minutes. In our house, it's tacos. In its simplest form: beans, tortillas, and salsa. Done. Add some whole grain rice (I often make a batch to have on hand for the week) and sautéed veggies, maybe a little Cashew Queso (recipe on our blog),[12] and we are happy campers. Some of Mom's favorites are omelets and quesadillas, stuffed with a little cheese, bits of meat, and veggies. Grilled paninis: a little protein, a few veggies, a little sauce of your choice between two pieces of bread, grilled on a skillet with a heavier pan on top to "press it." Small, thin tilapia filets thaw and cook in almost no time in a skillet: just season and serve with a quick salad or stir-fried veggies.

~

Once you've got your menu planned and groceries in the house, a certain sense of calm comes over you. That is, unless the family dinnertime has turned into a stress-inducing event of its own, with cranky kids, picky eaters, power struggles, or emotional tension in the air. Planning ahead for meals is only part of the stress-reducing puzzle.

Once you get dinner planned, cooked, and served, how can you keep the whole experience of eating together as a family a positive, nourishing experience, rather than one that ends in tears, yelling, and oatmeal on somebody's head?

BECKY

Nourishing Food Memories and Habits

I was about thirteen years old, having dinner with my family, eating a whole spiced peach, which I'd stabbed on the end of my fork.

Before I took a bite, I said something to my father, and for added emphasis, tapped the fork in midair in his general direction at the other end of the table. To our wide-eyed surprise, the peach flew across the table and did a two-point landing right in the middle of Daddy's glass of iced tea. Wiping the splash of liquid from his eyes, we all fell into laughter. It is still of one my father's favorite stories to tell and retell.

Contrast that scene to this one, recently shared by a good friend of mine: "My younger sister decided at age four that she would refuse *all* food except toast with jelly. This lasted (she prevailed) for four years. My Scottish father sat near her chair, a yardstick at his side, threatening her for the entire time we were assembled. He also wanted near silence at the table, since this was how he was raised. If we did talk, we couldn't argue with him about current events or anything else. If we got upset and cried, we were banished. And we were *not* allowed to laugh. Laughter got us sent to our rooms with no dinner. This probably explains why I weighed ninety-seven pounds all through high school."

Another friend recalled so many tense family fights around the dinner table that he could hardly force himself to sit down and eat around an actual table, preferring food on the run or in the car where he could dine in peace.

Perhaps this is why my feelings about making dinnertime a pleasant affair run deep. I experienced fun, connection, conversation, and laughter growing up around our family table. Before we "gathered together to ask the Lord's blessing," the phone was taken off the hook (back when phones had hooks), and the black-and-white TV in the living room was turned off. Dinner was all about face-to-face connection ... and a lot about laughing. My friends loved coming to our house for dinner, and even now that we are in our fifties and my folks are in their midseventies, many of them recall how much fun it was to eat at our house and asked me to thank my parents for those memories. No one forced us to the table; we didn't want to miss the good times to be had there!

With this background in mind, I have never understood parents forcing children to eat when they are clearly not hungry or making them sit at a table until they eat something they abhor or sending them to bed hungry to prove a point.

Force-feeding or withholding food seems to me to be silly at best, cruel and abusive at worst. It's a good way to serve your kids a side of future food issues along with their dinner—especially when there are a dozen non-food-based ways to discipline and reward children that are not fraught with so much baggage. Because taste and smell are some of the deepest and most long-lasting memories, sticking to the brain's limbic system like taffy, we want to be very careful that our children's experiences with food are mostly positive and warm.

What Naturally Healthy Eaters Do

Researchers are learning a lot about naturally healthy-sized people who don't have food angst. They tend to eat when they are hungry, don't eat when they aren't, and stop eating when they are full—no matter how much food they have left on their plate. Many people order a meal at a restaurant, knowing they'll save half to take home and eat it for lunch the next day. When we are hungry, our body digests food better. The very smell or thought of food gets us salivating, the body's way of preparing to receive a good meal. When we are full and force ourselves to eat, there isn't enough room or enough stomach acid to do the job well. On the other end of the spectrum, when we wait too late to eat, many of us get shaky, cranky, weak, and headachy ... a result of low blood sugar. Once I get to this point, it is almost too late to go back. I may satisfy my hunger with food, but I could experience that low-blood-sugar headache and even nausea for hours after. The same is often true of children.

Most adults who seek counseling to get help with food issues, bad habits, and extra weight have to undo everything their parents taught them about eating as children. Rather than eating at certain designated times, they have to retrain themselves to eat when their stomachs signal true hunger. Rather than eating everything on their plates, they have to learn to stop eating when they are satiated and not overly full. Healthy weight people also start with smaller portions and add a second helping only if they are still hungry. They are the kings and queens of the doggie bag, trusting food to be there later when they can truly enjoy it. Healthy eaters don't have a scarcity mentality. I have met lots of healthy, balanced eaters who are also true foodies. They daydream about food — but they tend to wax eloquent about market-fresh produce or artisan delights in small portions meant to be savored. They get rapturous over a perfect truffle, enjoyed slowly, with a cup of freshly ground coffee instead of three Little Debbie snack cakes with a supersized cola. They don't generally obsess about junk, fast, or processed foods. They have discerning tastes, and don't mind passing up a Big Mac when they know they can boil up some fast-cooking angel hair pasta, add a little warmed leftover chicken or roasted veggies, some artichokes or olives or fresh diced tomato, a dash of olive oil or butter, a sprinkle of balsamic vinegar and Parmesan cheese — and sit down to gourmet home-cooked fare in ten minutes flat. With practice, cooking is often faster than it takes to wait in line for fast food that is going to sit like a brick in your belly all evening.

Many of our generation grew up having dessert at the end of every meal, so the main course was something to "hurry up and get through" in order to experience the coming sugar fix. Naturally healthy-weight people rarely have dessert, because they don't crave sugar often. They savor and enjoy naturally healthy food. A bowl of fresh berries with perhaps a dollop of cream is a dreamy, perfectly sweet treat. A piece or two of real chocolate with a good cup of coffee, letting it melt slowly over the tongue — is treat aplenty.

The healthy eaters I have observed look forward to meals made of a variety of colors and textures and temperatures. They often garden (or have access to fresh markets) and know their way around a kitchen. They think of cooking as a fun way to unwind. They savor their food and enjoy it without guilt.

They don't count calories or carbs, but they don't pile up huge portions. If they want a special treat they will go out of their way to enjoy exactly what they want — say, one slice of homemade chocolate cake — rather than a box of prepackaged chemical-tasting donuts.

If we know these food truths about adults, then why, someone tell me, are we messing up our kids by teaching them eating habits that will not serve them for a lifetime?

Tips to Avoid Tears at the Table

Drawing upon what we know about happy, healthy, normal-weight adults, here are some suggestions for helping children grow up to enjoy food without guilt, without overindulging, without starving or binging or purging, without dieting, without obsession or deprivation. In other words without all the issues our generation has battled.

1. Dance, sing, and smile when you're cooking

Let them see you enjoy cooking. Seeing mom always stressed out about dinner not only stresses them out in the moment too but perpetuates the idea that cooking is a burden. Put on a little happy background music, and let them see you smile and boogie while you toss that salad. Or if dancing is not your thing, try listening to an audiobook, an inspiring lecture, or a talk radio show. Or enjoy sips of wine as you stir and chop. Remember, if cooking is the chore you dread, find a way to pair it with something you enjoy!

2. It's okay to nibble

Because I suffer when I have low blood sugar and am prone to get shakes and headaches if I go too long between meals, I have enormous empathy for children with true hunger pangs. If children are really ravenous and dinner is more than ten minutes away, pull a stool up to the kitchen counter where you are cooking dinner and let them snack on what is healthy and ready. Visit with them this way and make it fun. Let them nibble on the veggies you are cutting up for salad, have a bite of just-cooked chicken, sip a tiny cup of soup, take a little bite of cheese, or snack on a small teaspoon of peanut butter or a couple of almonds. True, they might not be hungry (or as hungry) when dinner is formally served. But it is also true that they won't be fussy. Simply offer them a smaller portion for dinner. Even if they are full, they can still join in on the conversation while others eat. If they are hungry again, as they may be, before bedtime, give them a choice again of healthy bedtime snacks. Popcorn, whole-grain cereal, low-sugar pudding and oatmeal, or yogurt with fruit are good choices because they increase serotonin and help kids feel sleepy.

A word to the wise cook as well: feel free to nibble as you cook, if holding out is too much torture. Simply adjust your portion size when it comes time to serve yourself! One of my snacking rules is that if I am craving protein or veggies (like mini-carrots and hummus), I am probably truly hungry and need a bite of something healthy before I get "hangry" and shaky. But if I'm longing for a handful of Cheetos or a cookie, I can probably hold off a little longer until dinner. When I am really hungry, I'll even eat leftover steamed or roasted veggies, cold out of the fridge with a little sea salt and lemon or a favorite dressing—and it tastes fabulous. Fills me up just enough, but I am still hungry for dinner in thirty minutes. The same is true for kids. If they are really hungry they'll snack on raw veggies; if that doesn't entice them, they can probably hold off until dinner.

3. Teach true hunger signals

A friend recently told me that her daughter, age ten, is getting chubby, and she thinks it is because her daughter has three teenage brothers and automatically eats the same guy-sized portions they eat. "But I don't want to say anything to shame her about her weight. What do you suggest?" First I told her that children often "chub up" prepuberty, so not to worry too much about it as she may be heading for a growth spurt soon. The other thing I suggested was to talk to her about "health" versus "dieting" when making food choices. And instead of "portion control" teach your kids to self-assess when they are hungry and when they are full. You can say, "Let's start with just one small scoop of mashed potatoes. After you eat them, nice and slow, so you can really enjoy every bite, if you are still hungry, you can have another small serving. Sometimes our eyes are bigger than our tummies when we're hungry! But we don't want to waste food you may not finish."

4. Limited palette? Don't worry

If your child eats the same foods, from a small menu of "likes" —don't sweat it. If the foods are healthy and there's a variety between protein, whole-grain carbs, veggies, and fruit over the length of the day (or even the week), let them have what they enjoy as often as they want it. Most children have limited palettes of favorite foods, but over time and with help they will broaden their tastes as they grow. (See tip 5.) The bestselling book *Bringing Up Bebe* points out that in France, nursery-aged children are often fed the same sort of elegant meals, fully seasoned and sauced, as adults.[13] Rachel found that Jackson, even as a baby, enjoyed veggies that were spiced and seasoned lightly—the way she and Jared enjoyed them. (Maybe kids don't eat their veggies because they are too often served canned, bland, mushy, or without flavor.) French children eat three good meals a day with one snack, so they are hungry (but not overly so) when it is mealtime.

5. Let them participate

The best way to get your child to try new foods is to (a) let them help you pick them from a garden or pick them out from a farmer's market or grocery store, (b) let them help you prepare them, and (c) bone up on recipes and ways to cook veggies that really do taste delicious. Nutritious sauces and dips can go a long way in helping kids enjoy fruits and veggies as treats. While I was busy cooking, I used to let my children play with food — make "veggie creations" out of the leftover (throwaway) veggie and fruit peels and parts, using toothpicks to put them together. This playfulness helped them see plant-based foods as fun!

6. Keep it light

Conversations at the table should be upbeat and without controversy or criticism. One of the most wonderful things about starting a meal with grace or a blessing is that it sets the mood for gratitude and positivity. A great discussion starter is "Tell me the best thing that happened to you today." Or "What was the funniest thing that happened to you today?" Or "What did you do today that you feel good about?"

7. Don't force it

If a child doesn't like what you are eating, and they've tried it before and you know this to be true, don't force it. It's okay to keep offering it, as taste buds can change, but have two or three fast and easy alternatives to what is being served for them to choose from. If they are old enough, they can prepare it for themselves (such as a peanut-butter sandwich, bean-and-cheese tortilla, string cheese and fruit, a quickly scrambled egg, hummus and multigrain crackers, or a healthy smoothie).

8. Make new foods fun

Make eating new foods enjoyable for kids by pairing the experience with something fun. Do a "toothpick" snack lunch or serve several familiar items along with a couple of unfamiliar foods on kabobs with a dipping sauce you know they like. My grandkids love to eat bite-sized tapas from "egg plates" — the plates made for serving deviled eggs at Easter.

9. Teach abundance

Start kids with small portions and then if they are hungry, serve them a second portion. This saves on waste and teaches them that there's "always more" if they are still hungry. You want to foster an "abundance" mentality with children to help keep them away from unhealthy "scarcity" issues with food.

10. Don't use food to punish

Don't ever withhold food as a punishment. It is nearly impossible for a child to fall asleep hungry, and making them do so borders on cruelty. If they react to low blood sugar with headaches and nausea, you can induce sickness by withdrawing food. It also teaches them to equate food with a painful or shaming experience. Not good.

11. Only eat in calm

If children are misbehaving at the table, assess why this is happening. Are they tired? Sick? Overly hungry? Not hungry? Frustrated? The best way to calm a small child is often to remove them from the table or hold them in your lap. Say, "Let's wait to eat until you are feeling calmer, okay?" I've always found a warm bath to be calming to little ones. Try this, and perhaps some snuggle time and a book, and then see if they are hungry, once their system has settled and calmed. You can tell an older child, "Why don't you go lie down for a few minutes, maybe read a book? When you are ready to be calm and kind, then come back to the table and you can try to eat again. In our family we always want to eat when we are calm and happy."

Of course, mothers of small children need some calm dining time too. Don't feel that you have to eat every meal "as a family." Sometimes it's better to let the kids eat first, then enjoy a meal in quiet, alone or with your husband.

12. Discourage the hoarding of food

If your child is hoarding food, find out why. Sometimes children in large families feel (and many rightly so) that if they don't grab their portion of the best of the groceries, the other kids will eat them. If this is the case, give each child a designated Tupperware box for the fridge and/or pantry where they can save and store a portion of food they especially love for a time when they are ready and want to eat it.

13. Serve healthy, yummy desserts

Most children will quickly adapt to seeing a favorite bowl of cereal or oatmeal or cut-up fruit (with a special dip or whipped cream) or a bowl of frozen fruit blended into "soft-serve ice cream" as dessert. Or make cookies from a healthy, high-fiber, low-sugar recipe. A spoonful of nut butter with a drop of honey is a fast high-fiber, high-protein, sweet treat. You can even sprinkle it with unsweetened coconut or mini dark chocolate chips.

14. End mealtimes peacefully

If your children finish eating before you are finished, that is fine (more time for adults to linger and chat). But to keep mealtime pleasant and peaceful, teach children to (a) ask to be excused, (b) thank the cook for a good meal, (c) take their plate to the kitchen sink, and (d) play somewhere quietly while others finish their dinners. If you make the table a fun place to be, your children will grow to enjoy conversation and attention and laughter, and they will want to linger.

15. Nourish yourself well

Finally, your children will follow your lead in how they eat, so do your best to show them the best examples of eating well. If you currently have more of a sweet tooth than you want your child to have, then just don't let them see you eating sweets. Have your sugary treat after they are asleep. If you smoked, you wouldn't feel compelled to give your kids a cigarette; if you drink, you don't offer the kids a little sip of wine because you are having alcohol. Have your ice cream and cookies after the kids are in bed and what they don't know won't tempt them. You're giving your kids new habits that you wish you'd been trained with—and perhaps if you had been, sugar would not be such a struggle for you now.

⁓

One of the most loving things we can do for our kids is raise them with a positive, healthy, natural relationship with food. The best way to do this is to make cooking and eating together filled with fun memories. It's not easy, and it takes a lot of planning. But few things you teach your child will yield greater benefits than healthy food and eating habits, and also good old-fashioned conversation skills and a sense of humor. With my mom and dad as such an appreciative "audience," perhaps it is no wonder that both my sister and I ended up writing humor and giving entertaining speeches. And now my daughter is following the same funny path to success. As Michael J. Fox quipped, "The oldest form of theater is the dinner table. It's got five or six people, new show every night, same players. Good ensemble; the people have worked together a lot." By prioritizing this one thing—healthy, happy family mealtimes —you give yourself, your mate, and your kids angst-free eating habits, good health, more energy, better moods—gifts that will nourish all of you for a lifetime.

Chapter 9

Barbell Therapy

Nourishing Movement

*An early morning walk
is a blessing for the whole day.*
Henry David Thoreau

RACHEL

College was a really stressful, lonely season for me. In the middle of my sophomore year, a big relational dream shattered, and between semesters I moved into an apartment all by myself, my first time living alone. Even with a balcony overlooking the pool, a nice new clean space to make my own, and some newfound peace that came from moving forward, some days the loneliness felt unbearable, and the stress and heartache were still fresh. One afternoon, grasping for something to calm my nerves, I drove to a gas station and bought a pack of cigarettes and a lighter. I was not a smoker, never had been, but at this point in my life, I was desperate.

Once home, I went straight to my patio, lit up a cigarette, and took a small puff. Then another, a little deeper. For a moment, a wave of calm came over me. My thoughts focused fully on inhaling and exhaling. Breathe in. Hold. Long slow exhale. Then, just as quickly as the calm came, it left, and turned to nausea. The patio began to spin. I put out the cigarette and went to lie on my couch, very very still. My head hurt, my stomach lurched, and my mouth tasted like an ash tray.

Clearly, smoking was not going to be the antidote to stress I'd hoped it would be.

After that attempt, I turned to what I knew: journaling, praying, and reading the Bible. Mom sent me a stack of self-help books that helped me pass the time and shift my thoughts toward areas in my life I still had some perceived control over.

Still, there is only so much solitary reading and praying that a girl can do. Then one day, at our school gym, I saw it, a flyer for a fitness class, Ripped. Jeff, the manager of the gym and a fitness expert with the physique to back up his credentials, was to lead the group himself. He was at the desk when I saw the flyer.

"Is this class just for guys?" I asked.

"Well," said Jeff, "it's going to be tough. I'm not saying girls can't come; I'm just saying, this is no Jazzercise. Four days a week, we'll spend an hour in the weight room and an hour doing abs and cardio." He went on to explain that he saw a lot of "muscleheads" come into the gym, and he cringed watching them destroy their bodies with bad technique and no regard for heart-healthy cardio. He hoped this intense class, with a name like Ripped, would attract some of them.

I tucked the flyer into my bag and stepped up on the elliptical to do my usual leisurely paced jaunt while reading a magazine.

For the next few days, I couldn't get the Ripped class out of my head. I showed up the first day, hoping to prove myself tough enough to hang with the boys. But apparently the muscleheads didn't feel they needed any of Jeff's help. Standing around the bench press, waiting for class to begin, was me, a girl from Jersey hoping to get in shape for her wedding, a middle-aged staff member going through a divorce, and a skinny freshman boy trying to gain some muscle. We were the Misfits of Ripped, and Jeff had every expectation that none of us would cut it. But he also had no intentions of sissifying his class to accommodate wimps.

Jeff kept his promise. It wasn't easy—and he did not tolerate whining.

But every one of us stayed. And we got strong, like serious muscles-you-could-see strong. Along with visible muscle tone, we gained confidence. Despite his initial disappointment, Jeff grew to love his group of misfits; we gave him the sense of purpose he'd been seeking. And the endorphins, the friendship, and the distraction proved to be exactly what I needed to get through my own emotional rough patch.

Because I'd been a benchwarmer in all of my athletic attempts in high school, I was surprised to discover a real knack for fitness. As the Ripped class grew, Jeff asked me to help lead stations. Eventually he asked me to design and lead a class in the evenings (Butts-n-Guts) and to teach a cycling "spin" class.

On the weekends, Jeff would take any of us who were up for the challenge on a long run on winding country roads. I'd actually enjoyed running in high school but had never run more than four or five miles. To run farther than that never even crossed my mind.

However, Jeff would take us on long runs that lasted for hours and push us beyond what we ever dreamed possible. The empowering feeling I had the afternoon I finished a thirteen-mile run still sticks with me today.

The great thing about running is that whatever I put into it, I got out of it. I couldn't help but contrast this experience to a long-term relationship that was dying. No matter how much I poured into it, no matter how much I gave, I might as well have poured water into a deep black endless hole.

Not so with running. When you run every day, it not only gets easier, you can go farther faster. You see results and they are worth the effort. Our East Texas campus was covered with beautiful pine trees and lush landscaping. I got hooked on the high of running under the shade of these trees with the sunshine peeking through. I felt calm and clearheaded as my attention zoned into breathing, inhaling, and exhaling the fresh air.

Not only was I getting training and experience in personal fitness that would normally cost thousands, but I was also getting the best natural stress reliever and antidepressant known to man. All with positive side effects.

Confessions from a Former Skinny Girl

Until I started exercising, I'd kept relatively quiet and to myself. To my surprise, I started to get stopped in the library or on the way to class by someone saying, "Hey, you're that girl who runs all the time, aren't you?" For the first time, I was somebody on campus. Okay, maybe being known as "The Girl Who Runs like Wind under Trees" isn't all that much to brag about, but it felt nice to be noticed. Classmates started coming to me for workout advice, which provided a good conversation starter if nothing else.

Along with my newfound identity and connections, by the end of the semester, I was, indeed, *ripped*. I had almost no body fat, six-pack abs, chiseled legs, and a size-2 pair of American Eagle jeans hung loosely on my hips. I hadn't been this thin since sixth grade.

With the help of a counselor, lots of prayer, and free "barbell therapy," I had finally come to a place of peace in my life. With the confidence that God had a better dream for me, I let the dream I had been fighting so hard to keep fly away, like a caged bird into the open skies.

The last week of the semester on a warm day in May, I was minding my own business working out on the leg press. And that is when Hotty McHotterson, sporting a baseball cap and an adorable smile, sat next to me on the leg extension.

"Do you ever have those days when you just don't feel like working out?" he asked.

I might have literally swooned. That's all it took.

Well, that "pickup line" and then watching him later as he worked out his abs from the pull-up bar. His real name, he later told me, was Jared (though I still call him by his nickname with regularity), and he was a pitcher on our college's baseball team.

On one of our first dates, I reached across the table, gripped Jared's hands, and looked straight into his brown eyes.

"I need you to know something," I began. "This is the very thinnest I will ever be. I've never been this fit ... and unless my life gets so unhappy again that I have to bury myself in workouts to avoid going home to an empty apartment, I'll probably never be this skinny again. If you and I remain as happy as I think we may be, I don't imagine I'll want to spend twelve to fifteen hours a week in the gym, which is what it has taken for me to look like this. I want a life that I want to come home to."

Jared assured me he would think I was beautiful at any size or shape and pointed out he was likely in his prime as well and asked in return that I not hold him to his collegiate athlete standards.

It didn't take long before I was skipping my Ripped class in exchange for an afternoon snuggled up with Jared while he napped and I studied. I no longer needed to work out as often for my sanity. The feel-good hormones from falling in love were compensation plenty.

And now, ten years after that heartfelt conversation, I have a wonderful life that I want to come home to. (Or more accurately, since I work from home, a life I don't want to run away from.) My soft belly and jiggly thighs are ample evidence that I am utterly happy at home with my loves. And Jared, God bless him, has kept his promise. He looks at me the same way he did when I was a size 2.

Letting the Glory Days Go

As happy as I was in love, losing my identity as a fitness junky was an adjustment. Exercise was like a cool friend that found me when I was down and out, and made me feel like "somebody."

When Jared and I first began dating, I wasn't sure where I belonged when I started exercising like a normal person again, a few times a week.

Years later, I found myself "name dropping" my connection with my cool friend Intensive Exercise. Someone would tell me they were running in a half marathon, and I'd say things like, "Oh, I love to run. I used to run all the time. I'm working on getting back into it. Maybe I'll run the next one with you."

Why did I feel the need to explain that I used to be a runner and present myself as someone who was just on a little break but planned to get back on top of my game again any day now? I wanted to tell the Super Fit Ones that I was really like them; I'd just gotten a little off track. Even though I'd asked Jared not to hold me to that old fitness standard, I had a hard time letting go of the Ripped Rachel I used to be.

One day, after telling someone I was a former spin instructor (never mind that I hadn't sat on a bike in years), I felt pathetic. Like a grown man wearing his high school letter jacket to Friday night games, grasping to relive his glory days on the football field.

So I used to be a fitness instructor. I used to be able to run thirteen miles. Good. Great. But that's not me anymore. As a wife and mother and writer, I don't have the kind of time it takes to get back the college girl I used to be. To pretend otherwise just leaves me feeling inadequate.

That day, I vowed to quit saying, "I used to ..." when it came to my appearance or my workout habits. I look back at those days fondly. With the motivation of a great coach and workout buddies I learned just how far my body could be pushed. I gained confidence. And I found Jared. But as I told him on that date, I didn't want to stay in that life. Even back then, I had an awareness that I was in a special season: a season of healing, where being a gym rat and running long distances were a form of positive therapy. I thank God for that time.

Now, when someone tells me they are running a half marathon, I say, "That's amazing. Good for you. Can I come cheer you on?"

Nourishing Your Body through Movement

Earlier, we talked about making steps to make our homes more nourishing and organized, all the while accepting that if life is actually to be lived in those homes—especially with children in them—they will not be perfect.

Ditto with our fitness regimens, especially when we have small children in our lives. It's not easy finding the balance that keeps us healthy, allows for a good rhythm of exercise, rest, and nutrition, and gives us a well-nourished body. Here are some ways Mom and I have tried to nourish our physical bodies, in ways that fit our ages and stages of life.

1. Pick Something You'll Actually Do

Of all the exercise routines I've attempted during this stage of parenting a small child, the one I enjoyed the most was a challenge to myself to exercise in some way outside for thirty minutes every day of December. In a month where it can be tempting to stay in and snuggle by the fire, it forced me to get some fresh air no matter the weather. I would bundle Jackson up in the stroller or strap him in the Ergo carrier and go for a walk or jog, sometimes stopping at the park to let him play while I did dips and lunges on the playground equipment. If it was rainy, I'd take my yoga mat to our covered back patio for a long stretch and ab workout. Jackson got hooked on the fresh air too. He didn't seem to mind the cold at all. Like a puppy nipping at his leash, he would climb into the stroller and beg, "Go walk! Go walk!" He was like my own miniature personal trainer, keeping me motivated.

Summers are a different story. It is so blasted hot in Texas that I have a really difficult time motivating myself to go for a walk. Jared and I just signed up for a gym membership during a New Year's special. I'm especially looking forward to using it this summer when our schedules slow down, and Jackson gets antsy for friends to play with and I get antsy for some me time.

2. Make Exercise Your Reward

Sometimes all we need is a little shift in perspective on the way we view exercise. Instead of telling ourselves, "I have to go work out," I try to see the chance to get moving as a reward. I'll tell myself, "If I finish writing this chapter, I can go take a brisk twenty-minute walk." "If I finish my housework while Jackson naps, then I can walk him down to the park when he wakes up."

Before Jackson was born and I worked an office job, I would treat myself on Thursday nights to my favorite yoga class. The instructor, a flamboyant young man in his early thirties, was easily 250–300 pounds, all belly, just like a Teletubby. He was on his own weight-loss journey and had found yoga to be an approachable and doable way to begin the process. During the first class I attended, he introduced himself and assured us—by holding his leg straight up to his ear—that although he was bigger than your average instructor, he was both certified and qualified. While I must admit it was impressive, the scene gave me a little case of the giggles. Then about five minutes into class, while we were all folded over like a peanut butter sandwich—nothing but butts in the air—someone passed gas. And I wish I were joking, but I tell you the truth: at the exact moment the sulfurous smell wafted across my yoga mat, we were serenely instructed to, "Come up and take a deeeeep breath, iiiinn through your nose."

That did it. I was a goner. The giggles got the best of me, and all I could do was fold into "child's pose" on my mat and laugh.

Still, by the end of the class, I was completely taken with the whole experience. The instructor turned out to be so encouraging and kind, taking time to teach each one of us the proper way to hold a pose. At a job where I struggled with overwhelming feelings of inadequacy, the acceptance and gentle encouragement in the class lifted my spirits. At the end of class, in the dark room, I would lie on my mat face up, eyes closed, and let stress pour out of me. Often tears trickled down my face, dropping onto my ear lobes. Thursday night yoga became my reward for making it through the work week. I couldn't wait to get off work to go.

BECKY

Often couples are able to motivate each other to exercise. One small drawback of my marriage, however, has been that we do not have a person in our marriage who likes to exercise. In fact, we've often discussed what good couch sitters we are by nature. Every so often one of us will suggest taking a walk together after dinner, but the other can easily sedate that idea with the offer to serve up a bowl of ice cream and berries and snuggle on the couch while we watch a movie instead.

However, we've found a few ways we've been able to motivate ourselves (if not each other) to get off the couch and move.

Motivation for Reluctant Movers

1. Pair something you like with exercise

As I've mentioned before, I am *all* about treats. Some days I live from small treat to small treat, and nowhere is it truer than motivating myself to move.

I try to pair exercise with something else I enjoy to make it more fun. On pretty days I enjoy a walk outdoors as long as I can listen to a good audiobook. Having never mastered the art of the iPod, I borrow lots of books on CD from the library, put on my fancy fanny pack, and tuck in my Sony CD player. I look like a nerd, but that has never stopped me from enjoying myself. I have, however, mastered the art of the Kindle. I will enjoy a fairly vigorous walk on our nearby rec center's elliptical machine, as long as I can read at the same time.

For almost a year I paired "getting to the gym and working out" with seeing my good buddy Ingrid. She and I never run out of things to talk about, and because neither of us wanted to let the other one down, we kept showing up, day after day. It surprised me how fast I went from being totally winded, to rockin' that elliptical almost effortlessly.

You may remember my "get your house organized fitness routine" from an earlier chapter. On days when I really get moving by cleaning or organizing the house with gusto, I count this as a "workout" and give myself a treat for a hard morning's work. Usually the treat is a guilt-free nap around 2:00 p.m. Naps are some of my favorite rewards for exercising.

I will sometimes reward myself with a Starbucks on my way to the rec center, if I just get myself dressed in workout clothes and out the door. Some days I reward myself with a Starbucks *after* I've worked out. And some days I reward myself with a coffee both coming and going. When it comes to getting myself to exercise, I have no problem resorting to self-bribery.

2. Move to better your mood

Like most women I'd love to lose twenty pounds, but that goal has never been enough to get me on an actual walking path or to the gym. I discovered, however, what does motivate me to get up and out and moving: feeling happy. So when I read that exercise gives an immediate mood boost, I dusted off my tennis shoes and mounted my treadmill. Just thirty minutes of walking does amazing things for my mood and my clarity of thought. If I happen to lose a few pounds in the process, all the better! (Although I usually walk while watching the Food Network Channel, so who knows about the ultimate weight loss.) For now, I must confess, I am mostly walking for the natural high. In fact, I may put a sign on my treadmill that says, "Will Walk for Dopamine Rush."

Because the Vitamin D you get from sunshine is also a mood booster, walking out of doors when the weather is pretty will brighten your spirits even more.

3. Move for brain health

High levels of stress actually erode the connections between the billions of nerve cells in the brain. Even low-grade depression, if it becomes chronic, can actually shrink certain sections of the brain. But here's the great news: there is evidence that exercise of any kind is healing and restorative to a stressed-out mind.

Finally, there is amazing, fairly new research that has shown when a person exercises, even moderately, just thirty minutes a day, five times a week, it has an outstanding protective effect from dementia and Alzheimer's. And if dementia has begun, exercise can halt the downward spiral in its tracks. Some studies indicate that even if you have the gene for Alzheimer's, exercise helps prevent those genes from "turning on" and affecting your brain.

Let's be honest. There's probably not a person reading this chapter who doesn't already know that exercise is good for you. The key to motivating yourself to move, however, is unique to each of us. Beyond fitting into our favorite jeans, movement is also a mood booster, a brain tonic, an energizer, and a stress buster. Which one of those benefits tugs at your Inner Elephant the most? Keep in mind, too, that the best exercise is always the one you will actually enjoy and do. If you are social, then it is likely you'll stick to a plan better if you do it with others. If you are competitive, you might want to join a tennis or volleyball team. Love the energy of a gym or need the push of an instructor or physical trainer? Go for it! If you prefer or need more solitude in your life you might prefer moving to music or podcasts or audiobooks as you go on a hike in the woods. If you are a romantic and want more time with your mate, go on evening walks, hand in hand, with your Love after dinner; or learn to waltz or tango in a classic dance class. Or maybe you'd enjoy a home-improvement project to get you moving and bending and pushing. You can nourish your body with movement in dozens of creative ways. I urge you to try several activities until you settle upon one, two, or three that get your Inner Elephant off the couch and into the conga line. It may take a little trial and error, but you will find the routines that are fun, energizing, and personally nourishing to you.

PART 4

Nourished Relationships

Chapter 10

A Gathering
of Girlfriends

Nourishing Friendships

We cannot tell the exact moment a friendship is formed;
as in filling a vessel drop by drop,
there is at last a drop which makes it run over;
so in a series of kindnesses,
there is at last one that makes the heart run over.
James Boswell

BECKY

I am not sure exactly how the four of us came together as a circle of comfort and encouragement and, over time, became nourishing friends: Michele, Lucille, Lindsey, and me.

I remember an impromptu happy hour around a patio table in Michele Cushatt's tree-filled backyard. We'd each contributed homemade sweet and savory tapas to go with the wine: red pepper hummus with grilled naan, chips with homemade salsa and guacamole, and the best brownies I have ever tasted. The early evening reflected the perfection that is Colorado in the summertime: temps in the low seventies, no bugs, no wind, warm with just the right dash of cool. We chatted about a dozen subjects for several hours, and all of us left wishing we could do it again—and soon. We were all writers, all loved to laugh, all had a special love for interesting and delicious food. We'd each put in time behind mics as public speakers, adored reading and talking about good books. We loved our husbands and had lots of kids among us, ranging from elementary school age to young adults, and a couple of us were new grandmothers. Tethered to Christ already, we gradually became tethered to each other in a tangle of fun, supportive, interesting friendships that has outlasted even our mistakes, differences, misunderstandings, and all-too-human flaws.

Michele and her husband, Troy, were getting geared up to enjoy their empty-nest years, their youngest son fast approaching sixteen, their two oldest boys out of the house. Then, suddenly, three small children in an emergency situation needed a safe home and stable parents. Troy and Michele opened their home and hearts to these little ones, none of them yet in first grade. Because we had Georgie living with us at the time, and also had a seven-year-old grandchild newly adopted from the foster-care system, we bonded fast and deep over how to be loving, healing forces in the lives of children recovering from trauma. (Michele shares the joy and challenges of this journey in her book *Undone: A Story of Making Peace with an Unexpected Life*.[14]) Michele, as exotically beautiful as she is Tina Fey-funny, nourishes my heart by understanding how a fairly normal life can morph overnight into something crazy and all-encompassing. She and I keep each other laughing, even if the humor occasionally turns dark.

Lucille Zimmerman, also around the patio table that summer eve, is buoyant, sweet-natured, with the face of an angel. She's also a compassionate therapist who generously indulges my fascination with her profession. Lucille and I met a few years ago on Facebook, and our interests were so similar we arranged to meet in person. We lunched for three hours at a sunny Cajun café, talking nonstop over blackened catfish, iced tea, and warm strawberry cake. It is interesting that some friends who you've known for a few hours can feel almost instantly closer than others you've known for thirty years. Lucille's book, *Renewed: Finding Your Inner Happy in an Overwhelmed World*,[15] about self-care, has refreshed my soul time and again with its practical reminder to prioritize myself as I plan my to-do lists. Lucille, herself, is a living example of what a well-nourished woman can offer to those around her: she radiates peace and savors the smallest of joys with childlike glee. My soul is nourished just by watching her delight in the world, along with her reminders to set "limits" and "boundaries" and to "take guilt-free time off to renew your heart."

Finally, Lindsey O'Connor and I have known each other since our passels of four kids each were young. Our writing and speaking careers were brand-new, shiny things that both thrilled and overwhelmed us. In her recent memoir *The Long Awakening*,[16] Lindsey describes the joy of giving birth to her fifth child in 2002, a darling baby girl named Caroline. Then, in poignant, lyrical detail she describes how this blessed event turned terrifyingly wrong, as her uterus ruptured and she entered the netherworld of a coma. Her life hung in the balance for months. Miracle of miracles, she woke up from what she calls Somewhere Else. Though her recovery would be long and arduous, she was alive and still our beloved Lindsey.

I will never forget our first dinner out together a few weeks after Lindsey had been released from the hospital. She was still carrying around an oxygen tank at that point to help her lungs, which were scarred by acute respiratory syndrome, acclimate to life off a ventilator. Lindsey has always been petite, with Jackie O style and beauty. The trauma left her fragile and even more tiny, but only the oxygen tank and the tracheotomy scar indicated that she hadn't just walked off the pages of *Vogue*. We ordered a celebratory meal, and while breathing through tubes in her nose, Lindsey reached across the table for my hand, looked at me with great compassion, and asked, "Now, friend. How are *you*?" Though I hated to complain to a woman fresh from a coma, I wasn't, actually, doing very well at all. In the past nine months I'd experienced more major pain, loss, and grief in succession (including nearly losing the dear friend sitting before me) than I've experienced in my life before or since. Six or seven things that had happened in those months fall solidly in the top three of the Major Life Stressors list. And here was my friend, barely breathing on her own, having just narrowly escaped death, allowing me the privilege of falling apart in her benevolent presence.

I look back at that scene now as a metaphor for deeply nourishing friendships. Even as one friend is barely recovering from one event, she still gives what she can to her friend reeling in pain. Like Corrie and Betsie ten Boom helping each other to survive in Hitler's death camps, you share your precious drops of vitamins and crusts of bread with your sister. "Such as I have give I thee" (Acts 3:6 KJV).

Recently we four girlfriends met for dinner. We've now journeyed in and out of the warp and woof of each other's lives for several years. These past weeks had been both the best and the worst of times. Among us we were celebrating two newly released memoirs, one new book contract, two newly married daughters, and Lindsey's move back to Colorado from three too-long years in Texas. Raising our glasses in a toast, our shared joy doubled our individual happiness.

Then we shared our most current heartaches.

They asked about how I was doing first. I'd shared with them earlier in the week that George's mom had suddenly moved out and on with new lives in surprising new directions while Greg and I were away on a business trip. Though I'd known this day would come, I hadn't let myself think about it. I'd assumed I'd have more time to prepare, that there would be a gradual transition perhaps. Instead, their move out happened overnight, in an instant. And since we were out of town when the decision had been made, we'd not been able to say any goodbyes. After nine months of living with, loving, laughing, and caring for a child who brought so much sunshine into our lives, we were grieving a boy-shaped hole in our heart.

I took a sip of my wine and opened up to the place in my heart that was still fresh and tender. "The first day Greg and I walked into our too-quiet home after our trip, I slowly trudged up the stairs to George's room. I saw the fuzzy foot of one of the stuffed animals I'd given him sticking out from under the bed, a forgotten treasure. I picked up the little plush puppy, curled myself around it, then lay on top of his blue *Star Wars* bedspread, and wept until there were no more tears left. Then I walked out and closed the door behind me. I don't know how long it will be before I can bring myself to walk into that room again. Right now everything, everywhere, all over the house and outside in the yard, echoes with the absence of Georgie."

My friends shed tears with me, as they knew how much I'd allowed my heart to entwine around this little guy. As Greg says, "Becky, you only know how to love one way: deeply."

Another friend shared how she found herself embroiled in a legal situation she did not deserve or see coming. Another was walking through a heartbreaking situation with a teenager. There was deep compassion, tears standing in our eyes, hand pats, side hugs, sincere words of empathy and encouragement. Our shared pain seemed to halve our heartache.

The best sort of nourishing friends rejoice with us as easily and sincerely as they weep with us in our pain. They long to see us blossom and succeed; they ache when we hurt and struggle. Interestingly, you may have discovered there are friends who can rejoice with us but don't "do" sorrow well. In fact, many a woman has been shocked and hurt to find that a good friend all but disappeared when things got really messy or painful or tragic. Typically, these disappearing friends turn out to be people who haven't experienced deep suffering (yet), and at this point in their lives don't know how to comfort someone else with a broken heart. It makes them feel incredibly uncomfortable and inept, so they just avoid the whole scenario. In contrast, there are friends who can mourn with us empathically when we're going through trauma but have no capacity to sincerely rejoice in our happiness. It is often the case that friends bond over shared disappointment, but when you move on or up—you get pregnant or married or lose weight or find the career of your dreams—their envy inhibits their ability to fully rejoice with you. The best of friends, the most nourishing ones, will both rejoice and commiserate, as needed, with all sincerity … even if it aches a little to do so. When it works, friendship among women can be one of the greatest earthly blessings. When friendships falter or end, it can be one of the most painful human experiences. Accepting some truths about friendship can be helpful in walking through those times.

Even the Best of Us Are Flawed

Even in the best of friendships, nobody is perfect. In fact, I think it might be a great idea before entering into a close friendship for both parties to go ahead and tell each other their worst flaws. "I always run late." "I'm terrible about returning emails." "I snort when I laugh." "My life is so full of kids and job, that I may only be able to get together once every three months." "I forget things. I need lots of reminding." "I hate political discussions." Then mull over the flaws and decide if you can accept these quirks in each other and still be friends. Last week a young guy told me, "We're all crazy. It's just that some people's 'crazy' meshes better with our kind of crazy." I thought it a brilliant observation.

Because friendships have the potential for nourishing or depleting our lives, it behooves us to be wise about those we trust with our heart. Even when you proceed with caution and wisdom, you have to know that the best of friends, given enough time, may sometimes hurt you, and you may hurt them. Most of the time, with good-hearted people, there's not an underlying motive to wound the other; but still, it happens. Misunderstandings or hurts are going to be part and parcel of any long-term close relationship. Just as marriage is made up of two good forgivers, so it is true for good friends.

No "One Size Fits All Our Needs" in Friendships

Another observation about nourishing friendships: rarely is there an all-purpose friend who clicks on all our favorite channels. Some of us find a friendship like Oprah and Gayle, where they are truly kindred spirits and bosom buddies. But more often we end up with an eclectic assortment of friends who nourish us, as we hope we nourish them, in a variety of ways. Over my life I've had friends who love talking about writing and books with me; friends who motivated me to get up and meet them at the gym *before* 9:00 a.m. (a small miracle and testimony to the power of this friendship); other friends who double the fun of seeing a good film or trying out a new ethnic restaurant. There are friends who invite me to dive into deep, honest, and insightful spiritual conversations, and friends who make me laugh until I cry. There are friends I go to for objective advice, and friends I call when I just want someone to empathize with me, putting all objectivity aside.

God gives us friends who nourish our lives (and we, theirs) for a variety of reasons, and sometimes dear friendships last only for a season. These friends were sojourners for specific times in our life but not meant to be friends for a lifetime. Our lives change and friendships do too, as we move away geographically or emotionally for any number of reasons. That's okay too. We look back at these friends with affection and bless them. And sometimes they pop back into our lives—surprise! surprise!—with a friendship request on Facebook.

Nourishing Friendships Fill Us, Not Drain Us

The most nourishing friends allow us to relax and be our best selves in their presence. They don't try to impress; they simply express. They share their honest thoughts and invite you to do the same. Over the course of time, you both find yourselves mentally putting your feet up when you are together, exhaling in the comfort of each other's company. You come as you are and leave feeling better. If you have friends like this, cherish them.

If, however, you tend to feel drained or insecure after spending time with a friend, you may be in a toxic relationship. In some situations, ending a friendship can be a very brave act of self-care. Other times, it's best to gradually spend less time with a friend without making a big deal about it. In essence, downgrading the time and thought you give this person to less of a friendship, more of a casual acquaintance. Other friendships you value can be saved with a heart-to-heart. A long-standing or close relationship is often worth the effort of trying to save after a glitch: you may even want to ask a pastor or a trusted spiritual mentor or counselor to help you navigate hurts, forgive, and set up any needed healthy boundaries and better friendship habits.

Healthy friendships involve a fairly equal exchange of deep listening and vulnerable sharing, and a delicate balance of giving each other space and grace, while not letting too much time go by without checking in and catching up. There's a natural, balanced give-and-take to healthy friendships. When a friendship is out of balance—someone does all the giving or all the listening or all the reaching, while the other always takes and talks—it isn't likely to feel nourishing to both people, and probably won't last long.

Friendships, Like Flowers, Need Nourishment

If you don't have nourishing friends, you may want to ask yourself, "Am I a nourishing friend to others?" Even the longest friendships need occasional acts of thoughtfulness, touch points, to keep them fresh and viable. Going to their daughter's wedding shower, showing up with a casserole when they've been ill, emailing just to see how they are doing, commenting on how cute their grandbaby is on their Facebook page, sharing an article or cartoon or quote that reminds you of them. These are silken threads that, over time, bond us to each other like webs.

My mother, Ruthie, used to advise me to keep my friendships in good repair because life is unpredictable and sometimes harsh, and we all need friends to help us through to the other side. Besides, friends bring so much joy, keep us away from loneliness and too much introspection, pull us outside our small worlds into larger concerns.

Friendships of the nourishing sort take time, thought, and a little trouble. And few things on earth are as worth it.

RACHEL

When I was a little girl, I had a fantasy that one day I would discover that somewhere, somehow, in a land far away—I had a sister. I wanted a female who shared my DNA and "got me"—someone who I could fight with and share secrets with. I needed an ally who spoke "girl talk," who would be my forever sister-friend. To be completely honest, that longing for a sister never truly went away. I've given up the dream of discovering my long-lost twin, but I have not lost the desire for more girlfriends to call on when I'm having a tough day, or an extraordinary day ... or even a plain ol' average day. For no reason other than saying, "Hi."

My best friend, Michelle, is wonderful for this—we talk on

the phone at least three times a week; I can tell her anything; she tells me everything. We text each other the funny things our kids do (especially the things we can't freely air to the online world). We've known each other since we were ages three and four, when our moms became best friends. Even though we never went to the same school, never shared the same circle of friends, and haven't lived closer than an hour from each other since high school, we've remained close. In fact, we've never had that much in common: I was a quiet, shy book nerd, and she was the loud cheerleader type who came by her good grades without really trying. I kept the rules (on neatly lined notebook paper); she thought they were made to be broken. She was bossy, I was timid. Michelle has long straight black hair and exotic dark olive skin. I'm fair skinned and freckled with wild curls. Her powers of persuasion were so great that she once convinced me to put my head down on my mom's ironing board to let her "straighten my hair" by pressing it with a hot iron. (When Mom found out, she let us know, in no uncertain terms, that we were NOT to starch and press my sweet ringlets again.)

Despite our differences, Michelle is a lot like the sister God never surprised me with. We don't have to fill each other in on the quirks of our families of origin, because we were together so often we practically grew up in each other's homes. We share a sense of humor, and she's honest with me in a way that I imagine sisters are. She tells me when I'm being ungrateful or acting like a brat. She was the friend who threw me a baby shower, who camped out with our family in the waiting room until I gave birth to Jackson at 3:00 a.m., and who has come to all his subsequent birthday parties. She is my forever sister-friend, and I wouldn't trade her for ten new BFFs. Still ... I have my husband, my parents, and Michelle programmed into my cell phone's "Favorites," but I'm left with several blaringly empty spots on my speed dial. I'm resisting the temptation to fill them in with our favorite takeout restaurants, but surely I can do better than Veggie Lo Mein. I'd love to add another close friend or two who share my interests and passions. Maybe a friend who loves healthy cooking and lives close enough to swap meals every now and then, or a writer friend, or a crunchy mama friend who will show me how to master the back carry with my Ergo or who likes that my house smells like vinegar after I've cleaned ... but not so crunchy that she'll judge me for tossing in the towel and switching from cloth diapers to Pull-Ups when we started potty training.

Lessons on Being Vulnerable

I moved to East Texas to attend college, but I didn't live in a dorm and was going through a horrendous breakup about the same time everything else was also dying around me: marriages, beloved friends, my grandfather. Even our twelve-year-old dog, Daisy, had to be put to sleep right before the only real home I'd ever known, on the banks of a lake I loved, was sold.

It was all so much, and the accumulating real-life tragi-dramas so surreal, that I didn't want to unload my life on some unsuspecting college kid who was just trying to get through Marketing 101, or risk falling apart on potential new friends. So I kept all this pain stuffed inside, and somehow put on a happy face and held it together while in social situations at work and school. I made straight A's, was a stellar employee, and when people asked, "How's it going?" I'd lie through my pearly whites and cheerfully answer, "Great!"

In hindsight, I should have just taken the risk of scaring someone off with all my realness. I should have shopped around for someone who seemed safe, and shared one vulnerable truth. Then if that went well, I could have shared more, and she might have shared some stuff with me too, and we'd have both saved our sanity. There's probably never been a time in my life I needed a real friend more. I did gather some great acquaintances; but without transparency, there are no deep, lasting friendships.

Bonding over Babies

When I married Jared, who was starting his career as a high school coach, we didn't stay in one city long enough to develop close friendships. As I packed moving boxes to head to Jared's next coaching job in yet another city, I remember thinking, *When we settle down, buy a house, and have children, this finding friends thing will get easier. We'll bond over playdates and MOPS (Mothers of Preschoolers) meetings and laugh about spit-up and sleepless nights. It will be idyllic.*

And some of those thoughts came true. I do have more friends now. We do bond over playdates and MOPS meetings. But ideal it is not. Connecting with other moms on playdates is like trying to tie your shoe while riding a bike. Deep conversations are tough when you are interrupted every three minutes to help blow someone's nose or take them to the potty or keep them from sharing an ice cream cone with a strange dog through the playground fence.

I envy how my mom's close group of friends go out on lunch dates (minus diaper bags or packing snacks!) and just chat and eat and chat some more. And they may even share a dessert because they aren't in a hurry because no one is waiting for them to come pick up their child. I know that women pay their "toddler mommy dues" in exchange for more freedom that (usually) comes with age. Though with that freedom, my mom says, come hot flashes, skin tags, and chin hairs. Apparently every stage of womanhood has its price.

In any case, I really do love working at home and staying home with my son. I know this time won't last forever, and I am told by older moms that it passes in a blink, though some days — when babies are sick and nobody sleeps — seem to last a week. I love our laid-back days at home between Jackson's two days at Mother's Day Out. And I treasure any evenings with Jared when he doesn't have a game. And writing. I love writing. The fact that I get to write about things that interest me — as a career — is insane. But at this stage in my life, I have so little Jackson-free time that when I do get it, I need to write to meet deadlines. It is hard to even think of giving up three productive writing hours in exchange for a lunch date, when I may not get another precious three hours alone for days. And if someone offers to watch Jackson in the evenings, I usually jump on this rare opportunity for a date with my husband.

Empathy for the Awkward and Insecure

You probably would never guess, if you met me today, that as a young child I had selective mutism, a form of anxiety that renders you speechless, literally, in certain social situations. Though I'm no longer the female version of Raj from *Big Bang Theory*, I still have some anxieties when it comes to meeting new people or "asking out" friends. Take my thirtieth birthday, for example. All I wanted was to go out with some girlfriends to celebrate. I told Jared not to plan anything, that I was doing a girls' night. But when it came to actually coordinating it, I totally chickened out. All my friends are busy moms too, and asking them to give up a night away from their family to celebrate me ... well, it just seemed like a lot to ask. Jared and I ended up going out for dinner while his mom, Jackson's "Mimi," eagerly agreed to a last-minute babysitting request.

Last year, I met a girl at the library with a son Jackson's age. She was new to town, and we seemed to hit it off. Then she left the building, and I kicked myself for not making a "friendship move." To my surprise, she was in the parking lot when I was leaving. I brushed aside my fears that she'd think I was a stalker or worse, one of those ladies who walk up and tell you how pretty you are, before handing you their beauty consultant card and pressuring you to buy their line of skin-care products.

"Hi again!" I said. "I know this may sound awkward, but I'd love to meet up sometime." She seemed genuinely pleased, and we exchanged cards and made vague promises to connect.

That was eight months ago. The card is still in my purse, untouched. Not wanting to come off too strong, I'd hoped she'd make the first move. Apparently playing hard-to-get may not be the best approach to making new connections. In fact, I'm realizing that women who take the more proactive (and vulnerable) role in reaching out to others, seem to be having the most fun.

Feel the Fear — and Make Friends Anyway

"Life was easier when playdates were set up for us," wrote Rachel Bertsche in *MWF Seeking BFF: My Yearlong Search for a New Best Friend*.[17] This might explain why some of my favorite friends are from Colorado. When I go to visit Mom for a weekend, she schedules girls' nights and playdates and dinner parties, and invites over young-mom-friends from church, women whose company she knows I'll enjoy. She's always spot-on, and I always have a great time. Now if only my mother lived near me and would coordinate all my playdates for me, life truly would be easier.

In the absence of Mom, though, I've been making intentional steps the last few months toward making friendship a priority. When I opened my eyes and started searching, I realized I had ample opportunity right in front of me. Low-hanging friendship fruit, ripe for the picking.

I recently arranged to have a sleepover with a fellow mom-writer, Erin, whom I've only met online. (Have I mentioned I'm an all-or-nothing personality?) Erin had invited me to speak at her MOPS group in Austin, which is four hours away, and when she asked if I'd like to come and bring Jackson the night before and stay with her, I did not back away shyly but instead took her up on the offer with enthusiasm.

"It's totally geeky how excited I am about this," I squealed to Jared packing my bag for the trip. As a coach and former baseball player, he's never had a shortage of buddies. He walks in the door most days with the phone to his ear, gabbing with one of the guys on staff. "What do you guys possibly have to talk about after working all day together?" I ask him, teasingly, even as a part of me envies the kind of friendship where you want to keep chatting on the phone after having just spent several hours together face-to-face.

Though my time with Erin went by all too fast, in the evening and morning we did get to visit with each other. I got an appetizer of how much fun it was to connect with another mother who juggles writing and raising children, who values time for family dinners, and who thrives on schedules and lists. Not only this, but her husband used to coach high school baseball and football, so Erin even relates to the unique role of a coach's wife. And they are Longhorn fans. Jared bleeds burnt orange. We were a perfect friendship match! If only she didn't live four hours away. Still, we've already made plans to do it again, with Erin coming my way next time.

I made a list this morning of all the current acquaintances or friends living nearby who might be candidates for becoming a new BFF, or at least a really good friend. Today I emailed two of them (and one serendipitously texted me). I am going to meet Megan (the architect-mom-friend I met at Common Desk) at a coffee shop next week, where we plan to bring our laptops and work. She's pregnant with her second baby, and I can't wait to see her bump.

In addition to the coffee date with Megan, I've got a playdate with two other moms to visit one of their homes in the country. Among us all, we have five little boys who love tractors and mud and farm animals. It will be fun to be around moms of active boys, even if we don't get a lot of deep conversation in between chasing the kids. I need the simple camaraderie.

Finally, I made a plan to go to dinner with a woman who is close to my mom's age. (My mom always told me to never put an age limit on friendship. Her dearest friends range in age from thirty to eighty.) Rhonda is a healthy vegetarian who loves to cook and garden. A mutual friend introduced us on Facebook when I was looking for a local organic co-op. From my Facebook posts and pictures, she wrote to say that it appears I'm raising Jackson much like she raised her boys. She is an expert at finding the most adorable farm-to-table restaurants, so we're going to meet at one of them, and I cannot wait to ask questions and hear her stories.

Making these dates happen didn't come easily. Especially for someone like me who thrives on routine instead of risk. It means giving up some time with Jared, though to his credit, he's being a great sport about watching Jackson for me on any New Friend excursions. Playdates with friends can cut into Jackson's naps (and shorten my time to write while he sleeps). Even meeting up with a friend for a "shared work day" could easily turn into more socializing than working. Not to mention the vulnerability of asking someone out, knowing there's the risk of rejection. Still, I am determined to take more chances, to overcome my reluctance to reach out and connect, to prioritize and make more room in my life for good friends.

Because one thing I've observed in the women I admire who seem the happiest, most content, and well-balanced as they age— they have all cultivated and made time for sister-friends. And in so doing, I can't help but notice, they have truly nourished their own souls.

10 Tips for Making New Friends in the Real World

1. Start with low-hanging fruit

Write down the names of any acquaintances or casual friends who, given a little more time together, could potentially become better friends. Then take a deep breath, reach out, and ask to get together. If all goes well, follow up and ask again. Most women tend to overthink friendship, which may be why Jared has more guy friends than I have girlfriends. Don't over complicate it.

2. Connect with humor

Emily, a friend of mine, posted on Facebook, "I've got to get a better social life. I'm spending my kid-free Friday night Face-booking in the Walmart parking lot." Seeing this, I perked up because she's a MOPS friend I've wanted to get to know better, mostly because she always makes me laugh. Though I know she was probably just being funny, I jumped at the opportunity and told her I'd love to get together sometime. With her trademark wit, she replied, "Are you asking me on a date? My answer is yes." This is where the Old Me would have said something vague like, "Yeah, we really should get together sometime soon." Instead the New, Improved, More Proactive Me set up an outing and put a date on the calendar, two weeks from now.

3. Practice being present

To get over shyness in making friends, I found that one good way to climb out of your shell is to allow yourself to be more open-hearted to the world at large. When you go grab coffee, resist the temptation to hide behind a book or plug in your headphones. Sit and sip while you engage with your surroundings. Smile at the girl doctoring up her Americano next to you at the sugar and milk bar, giggle with the mom whose daughter is proudly spinning in her new dress and almost knocked over the stand of dried-fruit snacks. If you've ever worked as a barista it's probably no surprise to you that there are people everywhere looking for human connection. Coffee shops are like nonalcoholic, highly caffeinated, safe, and well-lit neighborhood bars. Where one of the fellow patrons might just be your new best friend ... or a nut job. That's just the risk you take while practicing to be more of a people person.

4. Join the club

There are groups that meet regularly for every interest you can imagine: writing, reading, cooking, parenting, exercising, dieting, cycling, gardening. And if there isn't a group, you can always start one. One of my acquaintances noticed our community lacked a network for breastfeeding moms, so she started one on Facebook a few months ago and holds monthly meetings at her house. Her father passed away suddenly last month, and the group rallied to bring her meals and help out with her twin babies and toddler. In just a few months, the bonds in the group are evident.

5. Go to class

If you're not ready to commit to a group, look for a class on something that interests you: gourmet cooking, Pilates, novel writing, or sailing. (Or a class on "Writing a Novel While Sailing," or "Pilates for Gourmands.") Most cities have some form of continuing-education classes at the local community college that are short-term, fun, informative, and inexpensive. Join a Bible study through your church, or find an interdenominational group through such national organizations as Bible Study Fellowship or Community Bible Study. Check out www.faithhappenings.com to find a Bible study for women in your area. Or find a fitness class where the instructors and participants are known for friendliness and fun. As a young mother, my mom met some of her best mom-friends when she signed up for a Mom & Me swim class at the YMCA with her firstborn baby. If you don't find a friend-mate in a couple of months, you can simply look for a new class or group to try.

6. Volunteer

You will find some of the world's nicest people are those who give of their time and heart to serve others. You can search online (again, www.faithhappenings.com is a great resource) to find areas where you can volunteer your gifts and talents to help in your local church or community. When you sign up to serve in a soup kitchen or the church nursery or go on a short-term mission trip, you can meet the most interesting people, from all walks of life. The things that often define us—our profession, economic status, religion, children's ages—are stripped away when we leave our labels behind and join up to serve someone in need. Sometimes lawyers get sick of talking to other lawyers about court cases, and mommies get sick of talking to other mommies about childrearing, and food bloggers get sick of talking about food to other foodies. Every now and then it's refreshing to escape our normal worlds to meet fascinating people while serving at a homeless shelter, produce co-op, charity store, or nursing home. Where does your gifting meet a need? Find that place, and give of your time, and as a side benefit, you'll meet some amazing people.

7. Attend a conference or retreat

You'd have to go to lunch about six times with someone to spend just twelve hours together. With my schedule, this could easily take me six months.

Retreats for women or professional conferences can be a great way to speed up the friendship process, especially when you can bunk with a few other women. It's like intensive friendship bonding. After a full weekend of sharing bathroom counter space, meals, and notes about sessions you attend, you'll either have bonded deeply or quickly identified a friendship headed for failure (or just mediocrity) and saved yourself six months of "courting" the wrong catch. Try to choose a retreat where the focus is on making closer, deeper connections with other women. Typically the facilitators will make sure you get lots of varied opportunities to get to know one another in a variety of settings, designed to take you from surface connections to deeper sharing.

8. Offer to host an event

At the beginning of the school year, I invited all the moms and kids from Jackson's Mother's Day Out class to our house for a playdate. Though none of them have become my new besty yet, small talk during pickup in the afternoons comes more easily, which is nice. I've also hosted a recipe exchange and game night for my moms' group. We've started a home group with our church, giving us a chance to both serve and connect. (Bonus: It encourages me to clean my house at least twice a month.)

9. Say yes more

Earlier I mentioned accepting an invitation to a playdate out in the country. This came from a woman named Kara who, as I discovered, was friends with my husband in elementary school. We connected the dots one day while she was cutting Jackson's hair at our local salon. When her serendipitous invite popped in via text message, to be honest, I was tempted to take a rain check. That week was jam-packed, and it would mean a long drive out into the country, but I've made a commitment to say yes to friends more often, plus I had a good feeling about this match. As it turned out, Jackson had the time of his life getting dirty and playing with their boys, and I also hit it off with the moms. We left with promises to do it again — and I have every reason to believe we will. In fact, I could see us still getting our boys together years from now. You might be surprised when you determine to say yes to more invites just how fast your social calendar fills up. And how many opportunities for connecting you overlooked because it wasn't "perfectly convenient." In fact, I'm pretty sure inconvenience is often a big part of the Friend Package.

10. Assume you're a "hot commodity"

I used to assume that when I met someone I enjoyed that, since they were so likable, they probably had their dance card full of friends already. Lately though, as I've had my eye more focused on the friendship prize, I've changed that assumption. Instead, I'm pretending I am a BFF hot commodity.

Research shows that women *are* looking for friends. It's not as easy to identify when the appearances, especially with the advent of social media, makes it look like we all have 800 friends. It's easy to assume, "Wow. I'm pretty sure they don't need Friend 801."

Perhaps Facebook should add something that says more about our true friendship availability: "Happily Fulfilled," "Seeking Companion to Watch and Discuss *Downton Abbey*," "New in Town—Friendless in Seattle," "I'm complicated … but worth it."

Because I'm active on Facebook and write a blog, people can assume I'm all friended up. *Au contraire.* We might be surprised how many Facebook profiles would read "Looking for BFF" if we were allowed to be completely honest. (And weren't afraid of attracting crazed stalkers.)

~

In this search for a more nourishing way to live, I've been taken by surprise. Writing and researching this chapter—the chapter I dreaded the most—has given me the most NROI: Nourishing Return on Investment. As I wrote about what Michelle has always meant to me, I discovered I do, after all, have a sister-friend. She's been adorably concerned that she might get replaced in my search for more BFFs, and that makes me love her even more. Her spot at the top of my speed dial, I've assured her, remains secure.

I also discovered that women all around me are in the same boat, grasping to find time and ways to connect in this post-formal-education, often nomadic stage of life. I've discovered that much of my moaning and groaning about lack of close friends had a lot to do with keeping my head in a book (whether reading or writing one), instead of looking up and out and offering myself as an available friend. I haven't filled up my speed dial with friends I can call "just to chat," but I'm getting closer. It takes time to get there, but I'm confident that I'm on my way, and I'm enjoying the process.

Chapter 11

Sandbox Happy Hour

Nourishing Ways to Parent and Grandparent

All these people keep waxing sentimental about how
fabulously well I am doing as a mother, how competent I am,
but I feel inside like when you're first learning to put
nail polish on your right hand with your left. You can do it,
but it doesn't look all that great around the cuticles.
Anne Lamott

RACHEL

Tears streaming down my face, I looked at Jackson curled up under his blanket, body limp in my arms, paci bobbing in and out of his mouth. He was absolutely perfect, precious, innocent. I touched my tear-stained cheek to his and whispered, "Mommy is so very sorry. I promise I will be better." I kissed his little cheeks and prayed, "God, please help me be better."

How did this precious innocent child drive me so mad? He couldn't even form a sentence, yet I had yelled at him. Yelled. At a child. *My* child.

No More Yelling

My anger issues weren't out of control (yet), and my outbursts were rare enough that I honestly doubt they were doing the kind of damage to a child that couldn't be undone. But I sensed it would only get worse as he got older, and as our family grew, unless I got it under control. By the time he woke from his nap that day, he was clearly over it, laughing and playing and hugging ... and being defiant, as normal. But I was not over it. I spent days mentally beating myself up. I knew that if I wanted to fully enjoy my role as a mother, I had to say goodbye to losing it on my child.

Not long after, I came across a blog post, "10 Things I Learned When I Stopped Yelling at My Kids." The blogger, who goes by the name The Orange Rhino, committed to stop yelling for an entire year. I kept the post in my browser for a week, and I read it every day. The first thing she learned was this: "1. Yelling isn't the only thing I haven't done in a year. I also haven't gone to bed with a gut-wrenching pit in my stomach because I felt like the worst mom ever. I haven't bawled to my husband that I yelled again and again."[18]

I wanted that. I wanted to never feel that pit again.

I picked up several books on parenting that shed light on development stages of my child, along with the changes in their brains. As they say, "Knowledge is power." Knowing that his brain was not developed enough for extreme self-regulation, but growing like crazy in the area of "extreme curiosity," helped me understand why Jackson cannot, for the love of God or candy bribes, walk through the garage full of power tools and old summer toys without fidgeting with fourteen gadgets on the way to the car. He's a human Curious George, and I'm mom "with the yellow hat" trying to keep him from turning every trip out the door into an adventurous plot with twists and turns and spills and broken bones.

I told my husband about my blowups and asked if he'd help me to keep a lid on it by asking me about my progress and holding me accountable.

I'm far from perfect, but I have kept my vow. I am doing better.

Except for that time he stuffed toilet paper down my bathroom sink and then turned on the faucet and let the water run down into drawers and cabinets. When I saw every toiletry item, makeup compact, and bobby pin I owned floating in inches of water—I lost my cool. Jackson got another tear-filled apology that night. Though I actually should have thanked him; it forced me to tackle a home-improvement project I'd been dreading. Thanks to him, my bathroom vanity has never been so organized, the chaos finally motivating me to toss out blue eye shadows and butterfly hair clips from the eleventh grade.

Some days are harder than others. Mostly, I've learned that the hard days have very little to do with Jackson. The hardest days are the days I have my own agenda. Recently I caught myself whining to my husband, "Why does Jackson always have bad days when I have the most to get done or had a bad night's sleep?!"

Um, duh. I have less patience. I have less energy. I have less time to focus on him. No wonder the bigger my to-do list, the bigger his tantrums.

Even the Great Bathroom Flood of 2013 wasn't about Jackson misbehaving. I was lying down because I hadn't slept well the night before. He asked me to help him blow his nose. Instead of getting up to help him, I gave him some instructions on how to get the tissue from the bathroom, then wash his hands when he was done. I heard him playing in the sink but didn't realize my instructions had been lost in toddler translation. "Put it here?" I remembered him asking after I'd told him to put the tissue in the potty. I can't say for sure, but in my foggy exhausted state, I may have given Jackson detailed instructions on how to flood the bathroom using nothing but a tissue, running water, and a desire for adventure.

One of the most powerful lessons I've learned in this journey to a more nourishing life is: When I'm kind to myself, I am kinder to others. When I pull an all-nighter to make a deadline because I didn't better prioritize my time, I'm no longer the only one who suffers. When I skip breakfast to catch up on email, I'm not the only one who deals with my hunger-induced midmorning moodiness.

Sandbox Happy Hour and Other Win-Win Ways to Parent

One of the lessons I learned from cooking with Jackson was that finding or creating common interests with your children is vitally important to being a more joyful parent. I cannot engage with lawn-mower play all day, but I can do *some* of that. Jackson cannot play quietly while I write all day. He can do exactly two minutes of that. I've found my happiest and most productive days are when our activities intersect our mutual interests. For example:

He plays with his tractors in the dirt "plowing" my veggie garden.

He plays with bubbles in the sink, while I do dishes.

He uses the attachments on my vacuum (his "blower") to help me clean house.

He "saws" cauliflower for me to put in the stir-fry.

He enjoys a ride in the stroller and a visit to the park while I exercise.

We play hide-and-seek. (He "hides" in the same place every time, while I pretend to look all over the house for him while returning stray objects to their rightful place in the house.)

He learns a new dance move while I get to share classic hits.

I try my best to do tasks that take my full concentration — writing or computer work — while he's happily occupied, asleep, or at Mother's Day Out.

Last August, when football season started up (the season when Daddy works seven long days per week, while my patience steadily goes south), I started an evening tradition. Around five p.m., when the sun went behind our neighbor's rooftop and the Texas heat became tolerable, I would call it a day for my to-do list, pour a refreshing beverage, and head to the sandbox, where I'd sit and wiggle my toes in the sand, watching Jackson build sandcastles — me sipping, him sifting — until Daddy came home or the sun went down, whichever came first. Sandbox Happy Hour gave us both something to look forward to, allowing me to fully enter into Jackson's world. I let him lead us in play … while treating myself to a little beach therapy.

When the cooler fall temps finally put an end to that ritual, we took the beach inside and filled up my great big bathtub with toys and bubbles. He played, I soaked. We got relatively clean. It was a parent-child win-win.

Finding activities you both enjoy equally makes the days go by faster and more smoothly. You could even create a Venn diagram to map the interests for you and each of your kids, finding where interests overlap in any given activity. One mom-friend says she challenges her son in Lego building competitions. While she doesn't love Legos, the friendly competition excites her.

This same concept of overlapping interests can be an especially fun way to help your child connect with others. Grandparents, aunts, and uncles love the opportunity to connect with your child, so look for things they enjoy doing that might be unique and fun for your child to try. My grandma is a watercolor artist, so when my brother Zeke took an interest in painting, my parents would send him off to spend painting days with her. A win for all! I took Jackson to my dad's house last week for an afternoon.

"We power washed the windows, we vacuumed out the truck, we fed the horses, we organized the shed," my dad reported. "I don't waaaanna go!" Jackson cried as I carried him to the car. Jackson loves "doing," and my dad is the ultimate "doer," rarely sitting still. Plus, he has tractors and lawn equipment and tools—stuff little boys' dreams are made of. The best part? Knowing that the two of them had fun while I got a break!

Today I asked my friends on Facebook for some of their win-win parenting ideas, the types of activities they truly enjoy doing with their kids. The responses ranged from painting, crafting, dancing, hiking, and taking pictures of nature to sewing, taking picnic lunches to a nearby small airport to watch the planes take off, hunting for shark teeth on the beach, playing basketball and baseball, riding bikes, pulling weeds in the garden, and baking cupcakes.

Nourishing Rhythms

Jackson's Mother's Day Out teachers, who follow his antics that I post on Facebook, often jokingly accuse me of making them up. "He would never ..." "Our sweet Jackson? I don't believe it."

When I ask how they handle him when he gets obstinate or cranky, I only get blank stares. "We've never had those issues with him," they assure me. Jackson thrives in the classroom environment: the mix of structure with new engaging activities, the friends to play with, and the teachers to please.

It's easy to see that Jackson thrives with lots of planned activity that follows a schedule. Although our days are more laid-back at home, he does have a basic schedule: wake, eat, play, eat, nap, wake, play, eat, bathe, bed. I knew you'd be impressed.

I used to observe "uptight parents" who insisted on being home by seven thirty to put their child to bed. *How sad*, I thought. *They have no social life. I'm not going to be that rigid when I have children.*

And then I had a child. (Which could be the title of a whole book I could write based on my apologies for judging other parents in my childless past.)

Now I am the mother who will move mountains to be home by noon for Jackson's nap and in the house by seven for bath and bed-time. I quickly learned what most moms discover: children thrive in structure. It makes them feel secure. And when they feel safe and secure, they are more pleasant creatures to be around; which in turn, makes it infinitely easier for us to be pleasant in return. Giving our children some sort of predictable rhythm to the day nourishes the whole family.

Nourishing Careers and Passions

A mom told me today, "All the other moms in my home group do something creative on the side, like photography, blogging, or writing. I feel like I need to be doing something besides parenting. 'Learning to tango the feng shui way!' ... or something. Anything that makes me sound interesting. I feel embarrassed to admit, 'I just stay home with my kids. That's it.' Sometimes I wish I could wear a T-shirt that says, 'I Once Was a Teacher' or 'I Used to Be a Real Somebody.'" Another confided how much she wants to leave her full-time job and stay home with her kids, that she resents her husband at times because they cannot survive on his income alone.

It is the age-old question of how to balance our kids' needs for mothering with a woman's need to nourish her artistic passions or hone her career skills ... or bring in much-needed income.

It's a complex question, and one I'm facing right now. My mom was a happy stay-at-home mom, but even when we were very young, she found a little place to "tend her writing dream"—when she got her courage up to ask if she could write a mom-humor column for the local paper. They agreed and away she wrote! Making exactly zero dollars for her efforts. But it gave her the first of many creden-tials she'd need to move forward with a career in writing.

Eventually my parents moved our family of six to a charming lakeside fishing resort near a small town in East Texas. The job as "club manager" there was a twofer, requiring both of my parents to work. My mom's duties would be to take the job of clubhouse cook, catering meals for ten to two hundred, a couple of times per week, as needed. My youngest brother was just nine months old, my oldest brother age seven. To make it even more interesting, Mom accepted the job of creating, cooking, and serving gourmet meals with zero experience in cooking anything except weenies, burritos, and burnt frozen pizzas.

And so, almost overnight my stay-at-home mom became a caterer, keeping us kids busy in the huge commercial clubhouse kitchen, letting us make food creations out of piles of vegetable peels and pieces and toothpicks.

When my youngest brother was three and my oldest was ten, Mom decided to go back to college to finish her degree in education. She went just two days a week and kept catering part time. I was a quiet, curious little girl, and she'd sometimes take me with her to her college classes, which I loved. All of us kids were present and applauding when she walked across the stage with her diploma at age thirty-one.

We were all school-age when Mom tried a short stint at teaching but soon realized the long hours and energy consumed in teaching other children were stealing too much time and focus away from her own family. The family needed her income, but Mom came to a Family versus Income & Career Crossroads. "I knew I couldn't teach and be the fully present mother I wanted to be to you all." So she "retired from teaching" after "nine months of faithful service," trusting that God would somehow provide.

And the way He provided was a few jobs writing curriculum. And then, the exciting day came when she and my Granny got their first book contract for a book of humor called *Worms in My Tea*. When the book did well, Mom started to get requests to speak at retreats and banquets. The income would be significant if she could do it. The only problem: she was beyond petrified of public speaking. So she saved some of her book-advance money and took classes that helped her get over her fear, and in a couple of years she was a sought-after speaker as well as prolific author.

"I don't think I ever sat down to design my life as a working mother," Mom told me over the phone the other day, as I questioned how she nourished her art and her passions-turned-career while being a mostly-at-home mother of four. "I just took one dream and one year at a time. That way if the job or project went south, I could adjust and try something else the next year. I always prioritized being a mother first, but as you kids went off to school and got car keys and social lives of your own, I could afford to give a little more time to tending dreams. To tell you the truth, Rachel, over twenty years later, this is still how I operate. Greg and I will look at the budget and he may say, 'Okay, we need you to bring in about X number of dollars this year. How do you think you'd like to do it?' Depending on the year and on the current needs of our adult kids and grandkids, I may collaborate on a major book or do several editing projects, or as you and I have done the last two years—the most fun of all—write family humor again. It has always amazed me how God has provided just the right job for me that fits the year I am in. I do not look past the year at hand. It's been a blessed way to design my work and family life according to the needs of the season."

Now that I am about the same age as my mother was when she graduated from college and began her career in writing and speaking, I appreciate some of these lessons she taught me by example:

1. When your children are small, tend to your passions and dreams in smaller segments of time. As they grow and go off to school, spend a little more time nourishing your dreams, art, callings, or career.

2. If possible, seek jobs that allow flexibility with your time, work-at-home projects, or jobs where the kids can come with you now and again.

3. Know you've got to pay a few dues, perhaps even do some work for free, to get a foot in the door to the job of your dreams.

4. Don't be afraid to take risks. My mom wasn't a great cook but she knew she could follow a recipe and learn as she went when she took the job as a caterer.

5. Invest in classes that update your skills. Mom spent seven hundred dollars on a series of professional speaking classes and coaching. It was an enormous amount of money for her back then, and she had to save her writing pennies to do it. But she made all that money back on her very first big speaking gig and continued to inspire audiences and make a very nice living once she determined to conquer her fear and learn how to keep audiences in the palm of her hand.

6. Cut your losses when you realize you are in the wrong job. My mom thought she'd love teaching! She loved her college classes about teaching. But in actuality, teaching zapped the life out of her, which gave her nothing to give to her family.

7. Do yearly assessments and make adjustments that work for you: do more of what energizes you and makes your heart sing; take a hard look at your life balance; and if necessary, make hard choices that keep you balanced and nourished, that emphasize your well-being and your priorities.

8. Find good help. My little brother and I are still friends with the babysitter, Amy, who watched us when Mom did catering jobs and during one summer semester of college when Mom finished up classes for her degree. Amy was a lot like Mom, nurturing, funny, and slightly ditzy. (I remember surfing in knee-high bubbles in our kitchen

after she used a big squirt of Dawn in the dishwasher.) We loved our Amy Days. If you want to pursue a career or a hobby, you will likely need some help with your kids, especially if your husband works long or inflexible hours. Make peace with the fact that you can't do it all and then find someone (or somewhere with very good "someones") whom you fully trust, so you can be at peace while you work. (Whether that work is a few hours or days each week or full-time.)

I've discovered there is no one-size-fits-all formula for balancing job and family and your own sanity. Each of us has to find rhythms, activities, careers, and hobbies that work for us, that keep us feeling well-balanced over time. In essence, you have to design a life that fills you up so you have something to pour into your children.

BECKY

When I was young, I attended a church where the pastors and teachers were much more professorial than pastoral. I grew up thinking that all churches employed clergy who taught the Bible using an overhead projector, detailed outlines, and words like "discipline," "committed," "apologetics," "absolutes," and "rightly dividing the word of truth" (preferably in charts and graphs). So it may not be surprising that the parenting style emphasized in this church was authoritarian. The parenting book that was all the rage at that time encouraged a near-military approach to childrearing.

For example, I had some Christian friends who "disciplined" their children for the smallest infraction by "training" their little two- or three-year-old child to hold out his shaking little hands, while their six-foot-tall father slapped their palms harshly in full view of everyone. All this, they based on "the Bible's teachings."

But I got sick to my stomach watching their "biblical" philosophy play out in the terrified eyes of their precious children.

I stumbled upon my philosophical and emotional home among a group of mothers at a La Leche League meeting, while I was still pregnant with my firstborn son. They spoke with kindness and respect to and about children. Our group, made up of many kinder, gentler Christian mamas, encouraged more than nursing a baby — they believed in secure bonding, touch, responsiveness, listening, and intuitive mothering. The older children at play in the hostess's living room seemed so happy and sweet spirited. I left my first meeting feeling almost euphoric. I'd found my tribe. Finally, I saw a living illustration of the kind of mother I wanted to be.

It wasn't long before I became an anomaly at our church: the mother who birthed her babies at home, nursed them until they walked and talked, rocked them as long as they'd allow it, and preferred "lovingly redirecting them" to spanking. Now and again, out of "Christian guilt," I'd reread and try to follow some of the guidelines from the esteemed "parenting like a drill sergeant" book, but it put me in a cranky, adversarial, foul mood, and then I would start resenting my own children for their inability to act more like adults. Trying to create obedient little robots exhausted me, and at some point I decided I was a happier, better, more joyful woman when I strived to be understanding, kind, soft, and human with my children.

There was, however, one woman in a church filled with mostly left-brain engineer-types: a widow named Mary whose kindness was legendary. Mary dropped by one day soon after my first son's birth and gave me a copy of a book titled *How to Really Love Your Child* by Dr. D. Ross Campbell. "This is the book I wish I'd had as a young mother, Becky," she told me sweetly. "I want you to have it." As it turns out, Campbell's book influenced my parenting style more than any other. Dr. Campbell emphasized how to help your children *feel* the love you have for them. He taught "attachment-based parenting" before it was cool. His book is still selling well—over a million copies—after thirty-plus years. One reviewer's comment may help explain why: "This book is as loving and understanding to the parent as it is to the child."

Cha-ching. If I could give moms one piece of advice today, it would be this: when you read from the wide array of parenting experts and opinions, authors and other moms, *choose a parenting style that helps you to be the best version of you.* Choose a style that helps you feel like a more relaxed, fun-loving, kind, loving, happy, authentic, and nourished mother—and you will have found the approach to parenting that will help your children grow up to feel the same way.

Everyone's parenting style is different, but I'd love to share some childrearing tips and ideas that have made parenting (and grandparenting) fun for me. And when I enjoy children, I am a more relaxed, happy, and well-nourished woman as well.

Parent by Coaching Rather Than Controlling

By age four, one of my grandsons already showed signs of being a motivational coach, a miniature Tony Robbins. Even after I pitched a Nerf ball aiming for his bat and hit him twice in the head instead, he just rubbed his head and tossed the ball back to me, enthusiastically encouraging: "Come on, Non! You can do it! Remember: if you think you can, you *can*. If you think you can't, you *can't*!" And whenever he would get tired of coaching a grandmother with the athletic grace of a six-footed goat, he'd try hard to spare my feelings. "Maybe you should take a little break for now, Nonny, and go get Poppy to pitch to me. He might want a turn."

There is a lot to be said for the positive you-can-do-it "coach approach" to parenting. Your child needs to know, more than anything else, that you are on their team, their number-one supporter.

A good coach lets kids get plenty of time out on the field to play and mess up and play some more. A coach's job is to help them up, dust them off, and give them lots of opportunities for practice as they guide and teach.

Play Is Serious Business

It was a perfect fall afternoon when Greg and I arrived in Texas to see Jared, Rachel, and Jackson. I spent some time teaching Jackson how to catch grasshoppers by clasping his little hands— "quick, quick!"—above where the tiny insects hopped in the grass. He and his Poppy used their most manly voices as they steered dump trucks and back loaders in the sandbox. Over the next few days one of Jackson's favorite things to do was to crawl up in my arms and squeal, "Poppy coming!" with a look toward Greg that signaled, "Get off the couch and play chase with me!" Play is the language kids best understand.

Researchers know that play is also serious child-development business; it is through play that children learn to trust, use motor skills, take small risks that build confidence, discharge fears (and energy), and learn to self-soothe. And when your child plays alongside you, their little brains bond with, trust, and learn to love you.

In the marvelous book *Playful Parenting*, Lawrence J. Cohen writes,

> Playful Parenting can be ... the long-sought bridge back to that deep emotional bond between parent and child. Play, with all its exuberance and delighted togetherness, can ease the stress of parenting. Playful Parenting is a way to enter the child's world, on the child's terms, in order to foster closeness, confidence, and connection. When all is well in their world, play is an expansive vista where children are joyful, engaged, cooperative, and creative. Play is also the way that children

make the world their own, exploring, making sense of all their new experiences, and recovering from life's upsets.[19]

I can hear you groaning from here. "Great. In addition to all the other parenting duties I have, how many mind-numbing games of Candy Land do I now have to stop and play?" Do not despair, there are hundreds of ways you can play and bond with your child that don't make you want to repeatedly hit your head against the wall in boredom as Rachel pointed out earlier in this chapter.

Speaking Fluent "Child-eze"

I recently enjoyed my first phone chat with Jackson, age two and a half. The phone rang, and when I said, "Hello?" a little munchkin voice answered, "Hi, Nonny!" Jackson and I had a nice little talk about his upcoming role in a wedding that weekend.

"Are you going to be a ring bearer?" I asked.

"Yeth!" he said.

"What does a ring bearer do?" I asked.

"ROOARRR!" he answered ... and then the line went dead, leaving me laughing as I realized he thought he was going to be a ring "bear." In a few seconds, my cell phone rang again. "Hi, Nonny," Jackson said cheerfully from his end of the phone. "I hang-ded up on you." From there we finished our chat properly with goodbyes and I love yous.

When I was last with Jackson in person, I volunteered to read to him and rock him to sleep. But after the first book he turned around from his perch on my lap, took his paci out, and said matter-of-factly, "No more books. Let's talk."

"Okay," I said, "that sounds fun. What would you like to talk about?"

"Uhhhmmm," he thought. "The beach!"

So for the next twenty minutes Jackson chatted it up about crabs and fishes and turtles and sand and memories of an oceanside summer vacation with his parents and his Mimi and Pop (Jared's parents). He would also pause, politely, to ask me questions. "Does Nonny like beach?"

"Oh, yes, I love the beach!"

"Oh!" Pause. "Does Poppy like beach?"

"Yes, he loves it too. He likes the sound of waves going crash-hhhh, crashhhh, crashhhh."

"Crassshhhhh, crasshhhh, crassshhhh?" he mimicked back to me, perfectly.

"Yes."

"I like waves too. Mimi likes waves ..."

And on and on and on we talked in this vein, Jackson in his happy world of focused attention, remembering good times, and also, like a good conversationalist, volleying questions to me as well. It was easy to tell that Jared and Rachel had given their son lots of conversational practice and attention.

When we deeply listen to a child, whether we are rocking a two-year-old or taking a hike with a twenty-two-year-old adult child, these relaxed conversations fill their "love cup" in ways that pay fabulous relational dividends. Focused conversations bond a child to parent and deposit lots and lots of "love points" in the relational bank. Just as married couples who feel connected tend to have more patience with minor irritations, children also tend to behave so much better when they feel connected to you by regularly feeling heard and understood. When you help kids feel they have a voice, and that their voice matters to you, watch how their behavior and desire to please go up.

A Parent's Secret Weapon: Storytelling

My cousin Jamie is a genius with children. She is a professional nanny who puts Mary Poppins to shame. Her secret? Her spoonful of sugar? Creative storytelling.

In discussing creative childrearing, Jamie told me how she invents larger-than-life imaginary characters to make a point, while simultaneously keeping kids entertained. For example, she might call a disobedient antagonist something like Oh No Billy. Whatever naughty things her charges might think to do, she lets them know that Oh No Billy could do it a hundred times worse. When the children sense that Jamie is about to launch into an Oh No Billy story, they immediately stop disruptive behavior as they tune in, all ears, for the latest installment of Billy's crazy, horrible, terrible, wild antics.

Let's say, for example, that a child is kicking the back of the driver's seat as Jamie is ferrying them about town. Jamie might say, "Hmmm, hmm, hmmm. I just remembered a time when Oh No Billy would not stop kicking the seats in the car."

Kicking immediately stops. Child is all ears. "What did he do?" the child will ask.

Jamie will draw the story out for effect. "Oh, dear. I don't know if I should tell you. It's pretty terrible."

By now the child is all but begging for the story. So Jamie warms to her tall tale. "Nanny had asked Oh No Billy to please stop kicking—not once, not twice, but three times! Can you believe that?"

At this point the child's eyes are wide, caught up in the tale, saying, "I wouldn't do that. I obey *my* Nanny."

"Well, that's a good thing. Because the fourth time Billy kicked the back of his Nanny's seat, his foot went right through the seat, and kicked his poor Nanny out of the window, up into the air, where she finally landed on top of an apple tree ..." and on the tall tale will go, as far as Jamie's imagination and her little charge's attention will take them.

Jamie explains, "What never ceases to tickle me is that the young children never seem to make the obvious connection that I made up the story to help correct their current misbehavior. They get so caught up in the entertainment they forget about being naughty and absorb the 'moral of the story' through the returning character of Oh No Billy."

If you have a knack for spinning a yarn, trust me, you can hold a whole room full of misbehaving children in the palm of your hand.

You can also use storytelling in ways that calm childhood fears or traumas. When Georgie lived with us, he somehow became convinced that Big Foot lived in our basement. Logic proved hopeless in helping to assuage his fears. Finally I came upon the idea of enlisting his help in making up funny stories about Big Foot. Big Foot getting in Nonny's closet and wearing her clothes. Big Foot putting on Nonny's red lipstick. Big Foot making a surprise visit to George's kindergarten class and riding George's bicycle home. George would add to the funny tales and eventually began to see Big Foot as a gentle, funny comical character more like Harry from *Harry and the Hendersons* than some hairy, scary, malicious monster.

George would beg me to tell him stories of all kinds: funny stories about his Uncle Gabe as a little boy, Bible stories of Joseph and David and Jesus. Stories of nonsense or adventure. Then came the night that George announced that he would like to "take over" story time. He explained, kindly but honestly, that my stories were not quite as exciting as the ones in his imagination. So he became the spinner of giant tales, and I became an eager listener.

If you want to win your child's heart, alter their behavior, tame their fears, or teach them truths—the art of storytelling may be your new best friend.

Laughter, Mommy's Best Medicine

I've discovered that a kid will follow you to the ends of the earth if you make them laugh. And I will follow any child who makes me laugh to the ends of the earth as well. There's something irresistibly contagious and fun about parents and kids who enjoy comedic repartee.

Let's face it: there is no better audience in the world for adult silliness than children. As tiring as little children are, they give us regular endorphin boosts with their smiles, giggles, and funny antics. When my kids were young I scribbled the cute, funny things they did in a blank book. Over time, I began to look at everything my children did through the eyes of Erma Bombeck or Dave Barry, sizing up how the latest maddening or messy event might be funny if I wrote about it later.

So the day I found my two-year-old pouring the contents of a large box of powdered milk on the head of his seven-month-old little brother, who sat on the floor blinking like a bewildered snow baby, I grabbed my journal and jotted notes about what I was seeing before stepping in to clean up the mess. Those few seconds would buy me time to think, and often to chuckle, before reacting. Over time, searching for the "funny" in the frustrating became a habit and not only helped me find more fun in mothering, but eventually led to a career in writing humor.

These days I try to "catch and keep" the cute things my grandchildren say and do on Facebook, knowing I have a treasury of their "adorable funnies" to reread, enjoy, and share. One of my favorite funny grandkid quips was when one of the boys asked me, very seriously, if I knew that TV could "rot your brain."

"Oh, dear," I said. "Should I turn it off then?"

He answered, "Yes." Then, wrinkling his brow, he appeared to be studying me with concern. Finally, shaking his head, he added, "I just hope it's not too late."

Having George live with us was like having a short, bright, happy Forrest Gump in the house. He never tried to be funny; his innocence was complete and sincere. Which made him endearingly hilarious. Even this daydreamy six-year-old was impressed by how many things this grownup could lose or forget in one day. So he was always on his toes with me. The first week I drove him to kindergarten, I missed the entrance and had to loop back a couple of times. By the second week, he was sitting up in a state of alert as we neared the school. "Nonny! We're almost at the turn-in place to my school! Stop! Land ho!"

I cracked up, remembering he'd been watching a lot of *Jake and the Neverland Pirates*. "Georgie," I said pulling over into the drop-off zone, "I am sorry Nonny is so bad about forgetting things."

Always looking for a way to encourage me he said, "Actually, Nonny. You are really *good* at forgetting. You are a *great* forgetter!"

Ham It Up: Motivate Kids with Pure Nonsense

I love to ham it up with the grandkids in order to keep them busy and to motivate them to lend me a hand. For example, I once pretended to have discovered a big mess of "pirate's treasure" on my bathroom cabinet. (My pile of tangled earrings and necklaces.) It took no time for one of my four-year-old grandsons to volunteer to untangle, sort, and organize my pirate booty and put it in the right "treasure box" slots.

I have used many variations on the Nonny-needs-rescuing theme. I may persuade a grandchild to organize my pantry by dropping a hint of a treat to be found. ("Wow. I have no *idea* where I put those Oreos! Do you think you could help Nonny organize this shelf so we can find them?")

I may say something outrageous to engage the kids' help in cleaning up toys in the basement. "Hey, boys, do you have any idea where all these superhero figures go? I was thinking maybe they go in the toilet. Is that right?" Of course, since all little boys think anything related to a potty is high humor, the kids will break into giggles and redirect their Silly Ol' Nonny, showing her where the action figures actually belong. Organizing Nonny's Messes soon became their favorite game, as adventurous as any treasure hunt.

From an Old Mother to a Young Mom

About eight years ago I went to see an endocrinologist to ask when I might expect menopause to come my way. She took one look at me and said, "I will test your hormones, but just from looking at you, it would not surprise me if you remain fertile for many more years. You've got that 'I'm loaded with estrogen' body type."

Finally now, at age fifty-five, I'm saying fond goodbyes to my long-viable reproductive system. At long last it appears that this chick has run out of her almost unending supply of fresh eggs. Though I have been looking forward to this moment (no more periods!) forever, I have to admit there is something surprisingly sad about closing the door, firmly, on all chances of being a mother again.

Every time I see an adorable newborn or cherubic toddler on Facebook, a part of me still thinks ... oh, I wish I had one of my own, to hold and rock and kiss and sing to again. There are moments, I suppose, when all mothers ache to go back in time, to seasons when their children were young, and find them and love them and be even better moms the next time around. Even at my age, I still dream of my children when they were all the ages they've ever been.

This is a longing that quite frankly never goes completely away, for anyone who has ever truly loved being a mother. You do not want to pay the high cost of starting over again, but still ... the sight of a mother with child brings with it a twinge of something that's hard to name. For every woman who has ever loved and rocked their own baby, there's a wistfulness that goes with your memories of that precious golden blip in time when you were everything to your baby, and they, everything to you. Yes, grandparenting is the closest way to get to "revisit" the highlights of parenting again. But there's one vital and significant difference: your grandchildren belong to their parents. And though you are so glad they do, and it is as it should be, mothers the world over will always miss the joyously connected emotion that goes with mothering your very own chickadees.

So yes, young mamas, I know you hear this all the time and it is hard to believe when you are covered with spit-up or tussling with your toddler. But do your best to savor this time. Don't be in too much of a hurry; do all you can to slow down your life's pace to that of a little one. Because this season will never come again, and you will cherish it in your heart—always and forever.

Chapter 12

Secrets of the
Happiest Couples

Nourishing Marriages

Love doesn't just sit there, like a stone,
it has to be made, like bread;
remade all the time, made new.
Ursula Le Guin

BECKY

Greg and I do a lot of lay marriage counseling with young couples, mostly from our church. It's a long story how this ministry came to be because it is not something we ever dreamed we would do. But as we naturally and informally shared our stories with others, including our struggles, failures, and triumphs in love and marriage, our phone started ringing. On the other end of the line would be a bewildered young wife or husband saying some version of "We feel like we can be completely honest with you and Greg because you've been so real and we can see you've got a fun relationship. Could we … um … come over to your house and talk? We're going through a rough patch and thought maybe you could help us."

When we get a call like this, we'll set a date to meet. I'll put a cobbler in the oven and the teakettle on, and the young couple will show up at our front door. Often the bride's eyes will be red, and the young man will look disoriented and shell-shocked. We welcome them with hugs and point them to our comfy couches and assure them they've come to a safe place. Then drawing on the experiences, training, and knowledge Greg and I have gathered over the course of our lifetimes, along with prayers for the Holy Spirit's guidance, we dive in to do what we hope Jesus would do—bind up wounds, heal the broken hearts, and get them on a healthier, happier path to a joyful, relaxed marriage.

Sometimes all couples need are a few fresh ideas on how to do some things differently, a few tweaks in communication, or an understanding of how men and women think differently. Sometimes we recognize deeper problems that are, frankly, over our pay grade. Then we are able to refer couples to competent and compassionate professionals we trust. Through the decade that we've ministered to couples, we've learned that if a marriage isn't being proactively nourished in some way, by *both* husband and wife, on a daily basis, couples will begin to drift apart. In contrast, couples with the best, sexiest, happiest, closest marriages consistently nourish each other in several vital areas. And a well-nourished marriage insures that your "happiest place on earth"—now and until you reach old age—will be in each other's arms.

Nourishing Couples Flirt Wildly – and Never Stop

I laughed so hard when Rachel told me that Jared got her cell phone number mixed up with my sister's number. It is easy to do since they are both named Rachel. Among other cute flirtations, he texted his wife's "Aunt Rachel" the provocative question: "So what are you wearin'?"

Bless Jared's heart. He is the most polite young man I've ever known, the sort who's been raised by good Texas parents to treat women respectfully, to say, "Yes, ma'am," and open doors and carry heavy packages for them. So he was beyond mortified when he discovered his mistake, frantically dialing my sister to explain and apologize. (She thought it was sweet and hilarious.)

We all got a great laugh from the mix-up, but I was especially tickled. Because I knew that after six years of marriage and a two-year-old son, Jared and Rachel are still "haawt" for each other.

If I had to name the number-one difference I see between couples who seem to plod through their marriage, while others waltz to the tune of their love — it's that the second type started off flirting and never stopped.

Couples who flirt come alive when they see their mate. Their eyes light up, they automatically reach out, stand up, move toward one another; there is no one else in the room to couples in a nourished marriage. Like magnets, they can't keep their hands off each other, whether they are twenty or eighty. They are Nancy and Ronald Reagan, their eyes locked in a spell of adoration. They are Clifford and Claire Huxtable, looking forward to an evening alone, when the kids go to bed.

What does flirting in a marriage look like? It is a sly smile, a sexy wink, a love pat, a cute remark, a sexual innuendo meant only for two. It is texting each other a love note from across the living room or a loud party. It combines a sense of humor with a dollop of playfulness, and somewhere around the edges of flirting is the memory of, or promise for, sexual intimacy.

Flirting, in short, is what keeps the sexy feelings between you alive until the kids go to sleep or you finally have time and energy again for the real deal.

Nourishing Couples Sandwich Their Days with Affectionate Rituals

There are three times a day that are vital opportunities to nourish your marriage: when you wake up, when you greet each other after the work day, and before you go to bed.

Every morning since the day I married Greg, I've enjoyed the sight of a smiling man waiting to greet me, hug me, and welcome me to the day. (He rises at 5:00 a.m. most days. I don't come alive until 8:00 a.m.) No matter how morning-disheveled I am, Greg stops whatever he's working on and gets up to meet me at the bottom of the stairs, hugs me, and tells me how glad he is to see me. (I always fight the urge to say, "Really? Again? Looking like *this*?") Then he gently leads me to where I can find coffee.

I love our evening rituals just as much as our morning routines. Greg and I settle down in our ridiculously comfortable bed. We each reach for books or Kindles from bedside tables and read quietly—just inches apart—until we get sleepy. He usually succumbs to slumber before I do, but he always, always kisses me good-night before he drifts into dreamland saying, "Sleep well, my love."

Nourishing Couples See Irritants as Endearments

As you've probably gathered from your reading thus far, it takes a patient person to love a Becky. Here are two random status posts from my Facebook this past winter, glimpses of what it is like to live with me, day in and day out.

> I turned on the washing machine today and heard such a racket! Finally I went to check it out and discovered I'd thrown my iced tea, glass and all, into the machine with the laundry. The glass broke into hundreds of shards that punched tiny holes in all our clothes. I'm thinking of posting it on Pinterest. "How to Make Snow Flakes Out of Your Clothes—Using Just Your Washing Machine and Fine Stemware!"

> As per usual, it was an adventure getting to Phoenix today. I left *all* my medication and *all* my makeup at home. Painted my toenails red in a hurry when Greg walked into the hotel room and startled me. I ended up with red paint-smeared

palms and calves. (Wiped the polish on my palms, then tried to wipe it off on my calves.) And no fingernail polish remover. Pressed all the wrong buttons on the elevator so we went up when we should have gone down. With an elevator full of people. At one point I looked at Greg, who was not exactly smiling. "I know," I said. "There comes a point when this stuff is no longer charming or cute. But honestly, I am not doing any of it on purpose." At which point Greg patiently pointed out that I had only one earring on, having apparently lost its mate en route. People who dare to travel with me really should get some sort of T-shirt for surviving it.

For the most part, Greg gets a kick out of me, having settled into his role as a nonvolatile Norwegian version of "Ricky Ricardo" in our perpetual reality sitcom: The *I Love Becky Anyway!* Show. Because he really does love me, he has worked on seeing my irritants as endearments. Sometimes he needs a good night's sleep before he can actually see some of the wackiest things I do as humorous, but within twenty-four hours he generally comes around to laughing about it all.

To be fair, Greg has a few quirks of his own. For example, he loses the capability of speech, for the most part, after 5:00 p.m. A literary agent, he is all-talked-out after long days on the phone with wordy authors and publishers. He greets me lovingly but pretty quickly goes into his Hubby Bubble, "assuming the position" of relaxing on the comfy couch, TV remote in hand. We love road trips together, but we may drive for hours and hours without saying a word. Because I came from a family of Texas Talkers, the fact that there are long periods of complete silence in this marriage really took this Lone Star lady "some gettin' used to." In the South, there's a general feeling that if somebody isn't talking, it means somebody is ticked. But in the northwest, where Greg comes from, there's a general acceptance that if people are quiet, they are peaceful and content.

Over time, I've actually grown to love and enjoy these relaxed quiet times together when we say nothing at all. Thankfully, when Mr. Greg Johnson does speak, he says words every woman longs to hear. After a recent road trip when I wrote on my laptop and he listened to a book on tape, and we didn't speak for at least three hours, he took his earphones out and said with deep feeling, "I'm so happy. I love these long drives with you." Then he put his earphones back in, gave my leg a love pat, and we drove along in contented romantic silence until the next stop for gas and potty breaks. Not too shabby, once I got the hang of road trippin' with the Quiet Man.

Try to look at your spouse's irritating habits as if they were cute, funny, and quirky-but-endearing. A dear friend of mine, Tricia Lott Williford, wrote a poignant memoir called *When Life Comes Back*. In it she shares a story about her young husband insisting on calling a "trivet" a "trinket," and one day, after a heated back-and-forth on the correct name for it, he said, "When I die someday, you are going to look at this 'trinket' and remember me fondly." She let him know that *if* he died someday, she doubted it. Little did she dream that within months, he *would* die suddenly and tragically. And indeed, what was once an object of irritation has become a treasured endearment.

Nourishing Couples Each Bring
Their Own Sunshine

There's an old poem titled, "Blessed Are They Who Are Pleasant to Live With." The title alone describes Greg to perfection and why I find him the easiest of people to be around. Marriage is such relaxed joy when you live with someone who greets the day, and you, with a smile of happy anticipation. It's a cakewalk to be married to someone who is mostly optimistic in outlook, pleasant in mood.

We've discovered the most nourished marriages are usually made up of two people who take responsibility for their own happiness. Whether they were born with a pleasant, laid-back nature, or at some point made a conscious choice to take ownership of their outlook and moods — they are grateful, happy people who are a joy to live with and easy to love.

When Greg and I counsel couples in trouble, one of the things we look for is the possibility that one of them may be dealing with a brain imbalance. However minor this imbalance may be, we know that if one or the other struggles with depression, anxiety, anger, perfectionism, or an inability to focus and control their impulses, marriage counseling may not be lastingly helpful. So we encourage each of them to read *This Is Your Brain on Joy* or *This Is Your Brain in Love*, take the tests in the books, and then see if there's something they can do, as individuals, to improve their moods or their ability to focus.[20]

It is funny how often a marriage seems to "right itself" without a lot of counseling when each person works on bringing their best selves and most balanced brains to their marriage. This is why it is so important to nourish yourself, to find out what makes you blossom, and do more of that — because there is no possibility of a happy marriage unless you can bring a relaxed, joyful, balanced woman to your union.

Nourishing Couples Support the Other's Comfort and Happiness

Greg's desire for my comfort never ceases to amaze me. We were once on a walk in the hot Colorado sun, and I grew thirsty. We were still at least a mile from home. To my shock and surprise, Greg said, "Wait here a minute." I stood on the sidewalk and soon opened my mouth in silent shock as he nonchalantly walked up to a random house, knocked on the door, and asked the woman who answered if she might have a bottle of water or a disposable cup of water to share because his wife was really thirsty. To this day, I still can't get over being such a priority to someone.

What do you suppose helps people stay madly in love for a lifetime? I think it has very little to do with looks. (Look at Prince Charles and the real love of his life. She was never as pretty as his Diana.) People fall in love, and stay in love, because of the way the other person makes them feel about themselves. Someone who makes you *feel* smart, beautiful, talented, and kind (whether or not you are any of these things), and that you are their top priority, is pretty much irresistible. Don't waste time trying to impress your spouse; instead, spend your time listening deeply, noticing, and bringing out the best in the mate sitting across from you. When two people both do this for each other every day, well, this is where love blossoms.

Be careful not to go down the slippery slope of jabbing, cutting, teasing each other in dubious ways. Learn the areas where your mate is tender or easily triggered and vow not to go there, not even in jest. Every time you say and do things that make your mate feel valued and likable, it's like an invisible string attaches you to each other. And every time one of you says or does something hurtful, one of those attachment strings is snipped and cut. Whether a marriage stays viable depends on how many of those invisible strings bond them together over the years.

Nourishing couples strive to be a healing, rather than a hurtful, force in each other's lives.

Nourishing Couples Batten Down the Hatches and Weather the Storms Together

Life is full of challenges, and over the years a marriage will face every kind of trial from sleepless nights with a new baby, to job loss, to losing a beloved family member, to helping each other through hurts or betrayals. Not to mention the virus and flu bugs. But it is in the hard times that couples should do all they have the strength to do to continue to nourish each other.

On a recent and much-longed-for vacation — one week in Southern California, another in sunny Arizona — Greg and I both caught a flu of such misery that we called it the Demon Flu. We experienced exactly one day of sunny bliss by the pool when we arrived at the condo before we both went down with fever, sore throats, body aches, and a killer cough. On day seven of our mutual illness, I posted this:

> It is funny how being sick together pulls you apart in some ways as you grow quieter, more listless, lots less sexy as you wheeze and cough and blow your noses; but also pulls you together, like survivors in the flu fox hole. The one who summons the strength to rise, fetch water, pills, or soup becomes the Hero or Heroine, deserving of everlasting admiration and love. Last night, I thought Greg might cry with joy and love at the sight of me, upright, cooking a real meal, smiling and chatting from the kitchen condo again. (What he could hear of it with his stuffed-up ears.) When he brought home fresh veggies from the farmer's market on Sunday, he might as well have shot and killed a bear in ten feet of snow.

By the time we got to Phoenix on week two, all that remained of the Demon Flu was the killer cough and a newfound appreciation of our marital survival skills. Physical illness, not unlike emotional crisis, is made easier by each person doing the best they can to help the other when one of them is feeling a little stronger. And when one of you needs to collapse, be sure to lavish the partner who is caring for you with gratitude. Then you'll come out of the crisis having nourished your marriage in deep and profound ways.

In the end, a good marriage is not a given. It is designed and grown by two people, both committed to the art and privilege of loving the other more deeply and nourishing each other in big and small ways through all the seasons of life. And as Rachel will point out, it also takes a little romance. Your style.

RACHEL

My Kind of Romance

I was watching the movie *The Proposal* tonight. There's a moment when Sandra Bullock's character, a self-absorbed, closed-off, power-hungry editor is lying in a big bed alone, while her personal assistant Andrew (played by Ryan Reynolds), whom she has blackmailed into marrying her (it's complicated), lies on the floor at the foot of the bed. Lying there, looking up at the ceiling, she begins to share a series of personal, embarrassing, and vulnerable confessions about herself to Andrew. After she's finished, he gives her this gift in words, "Margaret, you are a very, *very* beautiful woman."

To me, this is romance. (Well, not the blackmailing part.) When we feel safe to put our guard down and share the real version of ourselves, to reveal our wounds, our struggles, and our utter silliness. When you know you have shown someone the real you, the you-to-the-core, without holding anything back, and they respond with "You are a beautiful woman," that is romance.

I honestly could go my whole life without Jared waxing poetic about our love or gushing sweet nothings into my ear. Mom and Greg, on the other hand, speak regular fluent "love mush" and find it delightful. (Our editor and I have had to explain to Mom, more than once, that even though we know the sweet nothings that she and Greg say to each other really happen, lots of people would think she's making it up. Either that or hate her for it.) Mom came by her romantic nature honestly, as her mom and dad were the original Romeo and Juliet of the family tree. She grew up around romantic mush for breakfast, lunch, and dinner.

I, however, am not really the stereotypical "romantic type." I don't like poetry or to be surprised. Sweet cards and flowers, while lovely and appreciated, don't stir up deep affections for my husband. Gratitude but not romantic feelings. Uber-sweet compliments make me feel kind of awkward.

I admit, I can be frustrating.

Jared and I made it far too long in our marriage before he realized his attempts to romance me were falling flat. I can't remember why it came up, but he was floored one day when I told him I thought we were missing some romance in our marriage.

"I try to be romantic all the time," he told me in frustration.

"No, you don't," I insensitively quipped.

Then he started naming all the things he'd been doing for me with a pure desire to please me. "Oh," I stopped him. "Wow. You *have* been trying, and I didn't even see it." What we had before us was a case of two different ideas of romance. He was doing the typical things that *should* make a woman swoon: buying me flowers, writing sweet notes, sending me flirty text messages, taking me to nice dinners, doing the dishes, telling me I was beautiful. And right now, I'm sure there are some women reading this who are hating me. I acknowledge that I have an amazingly generous man. I'm a lucky woman.

But I can't help that these things are not the buttons that, when pushed, make me want to throw myself at him in a fever of desire. Sure, they certainly prime the pump and add to my general respect and love for him. Deposits into our love bank. But the truth is, they don't *romance me*. If he wants to get me in the mood, the ticket is typically to get me talking, while he focuses and listens. Then he shares and I listen. You know, an honest heart-to-heart conversation. Or he can make me laugh or let me know he thinks I'm adorable when I'm silly. I'm frustratingly simple really.

Last night, for example, after Jackson was in bed, we were

chatting about our day and it led to a more serious conversation about some of the areas I'm having to give to God and how hard it is to not have any control of the situation. He listened to each of my words and offered empathy by sharing something deeply intimate about himself that he'd never told me before. As the conversation wound down, he reached across the couch and touched my shoulder and followed the outline of my tank top. "You're hot, you know that?"

"Thanks, babe," I told him, looking down at my black yoga points and stretchy pink tank top. "I guess you didn't notice I haven't showered and I'm in the same clothes I wore yesterday?"

"I did," he said through a breathy laugh.

"Oh ... well, don't worry," I assured him, "I didn't get dressed until three p.m. yesterday. It still had a solid half day's wear left."

"You do know it's nine o'clock, right? Your half day is up ... so maybe, you should go ahead and just ... take it off."

These are the moments that do it for me. The vulnerable. The silly. The flirty. The real. This is romance, Rachel Randolph style.

Sometimes we take for granted that our husbands should just know, by osmosis, what gets our love motor running. For years, I even let little feelings of resentment stack up, assuming he wasn't even trying to romance me. But Jared was trying and trying hard. I just expected him to read my mind, that's all.

Sometimes the most nourishing thing we can do for our marriage is to simply tell our men: this is what you do that melts me, this is how you sweep me off my feet and out of two-day-old clothes.

Finding His Kind of Romance

Along with not being much of a romantic, I'm also not great at giving compliments. It's a quality I am not proud of. I'm working on it, but I wish that giving praise to others came more easily and naturally.

My husband doesn't ask for much, but he really needs verbal affirmation. And to be fair, everyone needs to hear that they are doing a good job, that someone notices them and appreciates the little things. Last year I framed a print out that said "I Love You Because _____" and put it right by the spot where he keeps his keys, so he sees it every morning and evening. The glass overlay works as a dry-erase board. (Google "I Love You Because Printable" to find your own.)

As I notice something I admire about Jared, I fill in the blank. Over the year, I've written, I love you because ...

you never raise your voice in anger at me.

of the way you gently encourage the kids on your team.

of the way your strong calves look in athletic shorts.

of the way you assume your parenting role with Jackson, without me having to ask for help.

The more I wrote these little notes, the easier and more natural it became to compliment him verbally. The added benefit is that it helped me form the habit of catching Jared being awesome: looking for little things about him that make me smile.

And my naturally encouraging man almost always responds to my messages with a return compliment on the board. It has become a constant dialogue of affirmation between us.

If you want a man to repeat a behavior: make sure to give him lots of kudos for it. Most good men want nothing more than to please their wives. If you tell him, "I love how that blue striped shirt looks on you"—watch how often he'll start wearing it. And when he wears it, you feel loved. (Though this method can work too well with guys sometimes. A real people pleaser might start wearing that shirt every other day, until you are sick of seeing him in it. So use this secret at your discretion.)

Marriage Checkups

How did I find out that my quiet, don't-rock-the-boat husband needed more verbal affirmation?

Well, since the first year we were married, we've set aside at least one or two weekends a year to get away, to a hotel if possible, for our Marriage Checkup. It was during one of these "state of our union" conversations that he felt safe in sharing how much he needed to hear words of gratitude and admiration from me. I've since learned that most men need compliments from their wives because, in truth, men desperately want to please us. And they have no way of knowing if they are doing a good job of supporting our happiness if we don't tell them.

How to Do a Marriage-Checkup Weekend

The idea for a Marriage-Checkup Weekend came from a couple who helped mentor us before we married. From their suggestions and our years of trial and error, here's what we found works best for us:

1. We get a hotel (local, not somewhere too fun or expensive) and check in as early as possible.
2. We set ground rules (for instance, no belittling, cussing, or yelling; start and end difficult discussions with prayer).
3. We pray together.
4. We individually write down the things that are going well and the things we'd like to see changes or improvement in for the following areas of our life: sex, finances, work, the home (chore workload, home improvement projects), children, spiritual walks, communication, respect, affection, friendships, exercise, diet, hobbies, miscellaneous.

5. We pray quietly, on our own, somewhere to prepare.

6. We take turns sharing what we wrote.

7. We pray together.

8. We own up to areas in which we discover we've wounded one another, knowingly or unknowingly, and ask for forgiveness.

9. Together we brainstorm long-term and short-term goals for each of the areas mentioned.

10. We reward ourselves for all our hard work with dinner out and then come back to enjoy a night away in a hotel together.

If you're laughing at the thought of asking your husband to come away with you for a weekend just to sit in a room and talk about feelings, you might be surprised at how much your man needs this and will enjoy it. I can assure you that, typically, Jared is not fond of opening up. Yet he would be the first one to tell you how important these weekends are for him and for us. In fact, he usually initiates and coordinates them. Because he hates confrontation so much (and because I am sometimes not very gracious when confronted off guard), he really needs a safe place to tell me what's on his mind, in a setting where there are promises of calm resolution. And because my idea of romance is seeing what's been going on inside my quiet man's head and heart, there is always a sweet reward for him.

The first year of our marriage we did checkups quarterly. As newlyweds, there was so much to learn and figure out about each other that we really needed all four of them. Now with a child to coordinate around, we aim for twice a year, but even one getaway will do in a pinch. We never let more than a year go by before we take our weekend away.

Tips for Gettin' in the Mood

I've already mentioned that I'm not a romantic. Then I confessed to not finding it easy to compliment my wonderful husband. To top it all off, I also have a brain and personality that loves to make lists and stay on task. If you charted my "attention type" I'd lean toward the OCD side of the line, rather than ADD side. This personality bent is awesome when you need to get organized or focus on work that needs to get done. But it can be tough to let go of the list in my head, to be spontaneous when Jared has that certain look in his eye, to refocus and be fully present.

Knowing this about myself, the following tips have been helpful in getting me out of my own head and into bed.

1. Learn to love lacy little numbers

A pastor once told me that the secret to a long happy marriage was to buy either a new pair of panties or bra or nightie every week. Just one little somethin' that surprises him. (I've found this can go beyond lingerie—a sexy little T-shirt can do the trick.) I don't know that I need to buy fifty-two new sexy items a year, but I suppose updating my delicates drawer once a month certainly couldn't hurt. I have to admit, it's really hard to feel sensual in your worn-out everyday panties and your go-to beige bra with sweat stains. Something happens to a woman when she wears a new lacy little number though. She starts hoping she'll have a chance to be seen in it.

When it comes to shopping for special lingerie, the key is to find what flatters your body and fits well (which can involve a long, hard day of shopping and possibly a few tears). I've found, especially postbaby/nursing, I feel more comfortable in lingerie that's more structured than the flowy strappy lingerie that leaves everything "swinging around."

A creative woman really doesn't have to bust the budget on new items. Take a fresh look at what's hanging around in your closet or dresser drawers and throw together something instantly, casually sexy. Grab one of your husband's button-up shirts or old jerseys and slip on a pair of stilettos — *va-va-voom*. A tank top and silky shorts or cute pajama pants with something colorful and flirty underneath is subtly sexy without overpromising. Every woman needs outfits that say, "If you work at it, I *might be* talked into it."

I do want to mention that lingerie is just as much for *you* as it is for your husband, and if wearing it doesn't make you feel good about yourself or brings up old hurts, then please know you can have a full and satisfying sex life without it ... and a good husband will be understanding of this.

2. Shake what your mama gave you

Exercise releases endorphins. Endorphins are involved in the release of sex hormones in the pituitary gland. So exercise can actually increase our desire for sex. If you feel undesirable or feel a lack of desire, try exercising thirty minutes for three days in a row and just see if your desire for sex begins to increase. Listening to music that makes you want to shake what the good Lord gave you can double your efforts.

3. Read books on sex and intimacy and marriage

Early on in our marriage, I gobbled up books that helped me understand men and sex. Shaunti Feldhahn's *For Women Only*[21] was a great one for explaining men in a simple, funny, and honest way, including the basic differences between men and women and what makes them tick. (Jared also loved *For Men Only*.[22]) My mother actually bought me the book *What Your Mother Never Told You About S-e-x*[23] (some things really are best explained by someone else), and at certain junctures it was a helpful resource for, ya know, all the things I'm far too embarrassed to write about here. Let's just say that understanding an instrument makes it far easier and enjoyable to play. Jared and I also did a study based on the Song of Solomon called *Intimacy Ignited*[24] that gave us a better understanding of God's intent for sex in its purest, sometimes blushingly spicy, form.

4. Circle your ovulation dates on the calendar

God designed us to procreate, so when we ovulate (usually about two weeks before our period), our libido gets a little natural boost. Our body does a lot of the foreplay, if you will, for us. All we have to do is show up. If you struggle with desire and you are still getting your period, then you don't want to miss the three or four days a month when your body gives you some hormone help (of course, use discretion if you are using the natural family planning method of birth control). By knowing when these "I'm feelin' sexy" days will be, you can plan ahead to put the kids to bed on time, make sure you've showered, and send a flirty text to your husband that morning. Just as there are no bad days of fishing for most guys, most of them are thrilled with "pretty good average sex" for most of the month. But when your hormones are peaking, and you find yourself singing, "You make me feel like a natural woman," into your hairbrush-microphone … go with it. Enjoy an especially hot romp in the hay that night, an evening he can remember and smile about again and again. Nothing puts a spring in a husband's step or makes him feel more ready to "kill the bear" than feeling that he has pleased his woman by being a man.

5. Pray

I had a longer recovery than the average woman after giving birth and had severe anxiety about reestablishing our sex life. I was cleared by the doctor but was still experiencing a lot of pain. Add to that all the hormonal changes and not ovulating for months, and well, we were officially in a dry spell. When nothing else worked, Jared began praying over me until my waves of anxiety subsided. With time, my anxiety and pain both went away, and in the meantime God moved in our marriage and blessed us with a deeper level of intimacy than we'd ever had before.

BECKY

Getting in Touch with Your Sensual Side

Let's be honest, gals, even in the most well-nourished marriages there are times in your marriage when you are so tired you'd easily give up any number of mind-blowing orgasms for the bliss of one full night's sleep. There are times when you're awake with a baby (or hot flashes) all night, overcome with exhaustion, and you feel your husband's gentle hands on your back or shoulders, the international male signal for "I really want you," and you wish you could simply give him a pacifier so he too would go back to sleep.

But other than extreme tiredness or illness, many women struggle with "getting in the mood" for lots of other reasons. Maybe their body has changed shapes or sizes and they don't feel sexy. Maybe hormones have played nasty tricks on their former libido. Maybe she has forgotten how to nourish her sensual self: not just her sexy self ... but the self that enjoys all of her senses to the fullest. The self that lets her mind get carried away by Jazz music or takes a moment to soak up some sun in a sidewalk café or feels the sand between her toes as she walks on a beach or gets out paints and canvas and lets her artistic nature run free. If so, here are some tips for nourishing your sensual self.

1. Put on some music that stirs feelings of romance and the joy of being a woman-in-love. Or go to a concert, if that feeds your soul.

2. See a movie or read a classic romance that reminds you of the importance of passion. We love the movie *Moonstruck* for this reason.

3. Pause to notice your man, as if you just met him again for the first time. What are the things that melted your heart and made you want to kiss him?

4. Give yourself a beauty week. Indulge in a pedicure or manicure one day. Get your hair cut or try a new updo

(search "romantic hairstyles" on Pinterest for great ideas). Buy a new lipstick.

5. Shop for one accessory that says "romance" to you—that makes you feel sexy. If you've got a little money to spend, buy some lingerie, a pair of dangly earrings, or a soft scarf in a sensual color.

6. Just say yes. For some reason, the automatic response to a husband's overture for sex can often be "Not now" or "I'm not in the mood." I want to challenge you to just say yes and see where it goes. Quiet your inner excuse maker, or list maker, and give in to the pull of your lover's desires.

A final thought: There is no one "right way" to be romantic in your marriage, because it is made up of two different people. Every couple gets in the mood in their own special ways. This is where being a good "noticer" and not playing mind-reading games is essential. Throw away guidebooks and magazine articles on "What Turns a Woman On" or "What Gets Your Man Hot" and start experimenting, observing, and taking notes on the unique person God gave you.

Love and sex are messy, glorious things. And passion between a man and a woman is mysterious, as unique to each marriage as human beings are unique on this planet. My best advice is that in between the moments of babies crying and bills waiting to be paid and groceries to be put away—allow yourself to be pulled into moments of abandoned passion with the man you married, as often as you can. Give in to the tide. Let him sweep you away.

Whether you realize it or not at the time, a passionate escape away from the world with the man of your dreams, is one of the most nourishing gifts you can give yourself.

PART 5

Nourished Spirits

Chapter 13

Your Mind
Is a Garden

Nourishing Thoughts
That Tend and Mend Us

Surprising things can happen to anyone who, when a disagreeable
or discouraged thought comes into his mind, just has the sense
to remember in time and push it out by putting in an agreeable
determinedly courageous one. Two things cannot be in one place.
Where you tend a rose, my lad, a thistle cannot grow.
Frances Hodgson Burnett, *The Secret Garden*

BECKY

Over the past few years as Rachel and I pondered the subject
of this book together, I envisioned we'd write about "the well-
nourished life" while lounging at a seaside resort somewhere,
savoring lemon gelato. My unconscious thoughts went something
like this: "If we write about more nourishing lives, then our days
will be filled with a sense of relaxed joy, our relationships will be
peaceful, and all our hair days good. Because if we write about the
life we dream of—won't that be enough to make it come true?"

I don't know why I thought in this vein, when every book I've
ever written over the last twenty years has been accompanied

by severe testing on the very subject I'd so cheerfully (and often naively) planned to wax eloquent about. Why is that? I'm not sure, but I have a sneaking suspicion it is because God has an affinity for propelling us deeper than we want to go. He never seems content to let me get away with a simple face-lift approach to writing; He's forever bound and determined to do some kind of major surgery on my heart in the process instead. (If you think writing is a glamorous business, let this serve as a warning.)

A sudden and unexpected blow to the heart occurred during the year of writing this book that no amount of gelato, however cool and creamy, could chase away. I can't share the details of this unfolding saga, as it is not mine alone to tell and is still very much in process. Honestly, the details aren't important because there are a thousand variations on the same story of heartache common to womankind. We could all point to a chapter in our life's story where we experienced rejection, disappointment, betrayal, illness, injury, loss, death, hurt, unfair judgment, harsh treatment, relational strain, injury, sadness, remorse, failure, regrets. No story that's worth telling or remembering goes without its challenging or heart-wrenching seasons. The best lessons and triumphs and "happily ever after" endings most often seem to come to us while we are making our way through crisis and arriving on the other side — however exhausted and bedraggled — as better, wiser, stronger women.

Because I'm fifty-five now and have seen ashes turn to beauty time and again, I know God is at work, using all things, even the awful ones, for ultimate good. Still, knowing that the big "saga of our lives" will eventually have God's redemptive hands all over it doesn't mean the current "dailies" don't involve a lot of hand-wringing, mental ping-ponging, and desperate grasping for a daily crust of calm. Greg and I spent a good amount of time over the last six months thrashing about in the emotional quicksand of hurt and bewilderment, trying to help each other make sense of what happened. What pulled us out of the mire when one or the other of us started to sink too deep?

In a word: nourishment.

Greg and I applied everything Rachel and I have written about self-care thus far and then some. The worse the pain du jour, the more we focused on nourishing ourselves and each other. Even though we did not sell our house, I have been so grateful for the nourishing touches, the streamlining of "stuff," and the organizing I did a few months ago. Our home has been a safe nest of serenity in which to curl up, tend to each other, and mend.

Whether we are dealing with genuine deep grief, a really big ouch, or we're simply having a bad day or week, we've all experienced having our calm hijacked. Just as courage is not the absence of fear but the determination to be brave and move forward in spite of our nerves, genuine peace is not the absence of trauma but is finding our calm in the midst of turmoil, the presence of Jesus asleep in the storm.

A friend wrote today and said, "Even though you two are going through such a confusing and painful time, I'm encouraged that you seem to be finding your way back to peace and joy anyway."

I have always loved those two words together: "joy anyway." (Jesus referred to this as "the joy no man can take away.") There used to be a lady on our local radio in Texas who'd drawl a cheerful, "Make Your Ooooown Sunshine!" at the close of her show. It was just another way to say, "Find joy anyway!"

I could write a whole book on this subject, and perhaps one day I will. In fact, my editor and my daughter have chuckled at how often I start to write about one subject—then, within two paragraphs, find I've rabbit-trailed into discussing "Joy Anyway" or "Relief for Grief." One of the occupational hazards of being a writer (or speaker) is that what you are currently experiencing keeps popping onto the page, or out of your mouth, whether or not it is "on topic." I emailed Rachel yesterday, saying, "I believe I could start out writing about omelets and within two paragraphs be writing about how to soothe heartache. Perhaps my next book will be called: *Three Beaten Eggs in a Skillet — and Other Cures for Existential Despair.* But for now, I am just thrilled to have finally arrived at a point in the book where I can chat freely about what I'm most passionate about right now: joy anyway.

And where the best epic stories often begin, this journey too starts in a garden.

Your Mind Is a Garden

When Winifred Gallagher, author of the book *Rapt*, was diagnosed with cancer she was determined to find a way to rein in her thoughts so that, on top of treating the cancer, she wouldn't add to her suffering by ruminating over worst-case scenarios. Thus began an experiment in purposeful focus. Relentlessly, she redirected her wayward worrisome thoughts toward the things that matter most: "Big ones like family and friends, spiritual life, and small ones like movies, walks, and a 6:30 p.m. martini." In her book, Gallagher encourages people to live a focused life by "treating your mind as you would a private garden and being as careful as possible about what you introduce and allow to grow there."[25]

For years I've never understood what classical spiritual writers meant when they spoke about "soul work," but I'm beginning to grasp the concept now through Gallagher's metaphor of gardening. It takes hard work to seed, weed, prune, and tend the mind.

The apostle Paul wrote a lot about the spiritual art of taming the mind. He used phrases like "capturing thoughts" and "renewing the mind," and he encouraged the mental practice of gratitude and positive focus on things that were true, noble, right, pure, lovely, admirable, excellent, and praiseworthy (Philippians 4:8). Since "life is the sum total of what you focus on,"[26] the harvest of a well-nourished mind can be happiness, calm, freedom, and love.

Your mind can be like a private sanctuary, a secret garden when it is well nourished.

Do you know someone you admire who has wisdom, kindness, impulse control, balanced acceptance of their flaws and talents, and a healthy way of handling adversity or unfairness? A person who, when they walk into a room, elevates the very atmosphere with relaxed acceptance and joyful connection? A happy array of faces parade through my mind: my Nonny, my mom, my dad, my husband, my cousin Jamie, my daughter … and any number of dear friends I've known and admired.

Wise, delightful people have beautifully tended minds. They purposefully cultivate a rich, wise thought life through reading, prayer, good mentoring, music, and more — focusing their attention wherever they want to grow. My husband's wisdom comes, in part, from reading through the book of Proverbs several times, every year. His mind has been watered with the wisdom of Solomon for decades, and it shows in how he conducts his business and life. My lifelong beloved friend, my cousin Jamie, credits her peaceful wisdom with the years she spent in twelve-step programs, first in recovery, and the last couple of decades as a sponsor.

When we selectively choose thoughts that nourish us ("God is in control," "I can trust Him to sort this out," "He has not lost my file," "He saves every teardrop," "He and I can get through this"), we reap the emotions of peace and joy. When we are picky about the people we allow into our circle of influence, the music and movies and books we enjoy, the spaces and places we hang out, we are designing the mind garden that will nourish not only ourselves but those around us.

No amount of hard work or success, however, will provide us with a meaningful, joyful, and interesting life if we allow the weeds in our minds to grow wild: fruitlessly ruminating on past offenses or future concerns; fixating on a person who offended us and creating elaborate speeches of "How They Done Us Wrong";

or putting our joy on hold waiting for some imagined perfect circumstance.

Thoughts can sometimes be deceptive. They may make us feel good for a while, even righteous and spiritual. But how do you know if a certain train of thought is a weed or a flower? Here's my experience: when my mind settles "on things above"—I tend to feel more relaxed, expansive, loving, peaceful, and clearheaded. If, instead, after a bit of mental meandering, I feel angry, stressed, tied in knots, worried, or afraid—I know my thoughts are likely wild weeds. It's always easiest to stop a negative thought at the threshold of entry so I've learned to simply say to myself, "Not going there," or "Not planting that." Pausing the negative string of thoughts helps me to refocus and redirect.

Making Nourishing Thoughts "Sticky"

To create a well-stored mind you can seek out the thoughts, Scriptures, beautiful images, quotes, prayers, music, poetry, inspiring people, and great movies that nourish you. (And there's nothing wrong with a shallow but hilarious comedy either. I imagine humor to be like those enormous yellow sunflowers in the garden of my mind. Laughter is so healing and calming to my anxiety-prone brain.)

But how can you make the positive thoughts stick and stay?

Researchers discovered that negative thoughts are like Velcro; they are naturally sticky to the brain. (Wouldn't you know it?) This is why we can get a headache and automatically assume it is a tumor, imagine our demise, and get angry at our husbands for picking a new wife we don't like. And this negative spiral of thoughts can go down in our brain with almost no conscious effort on our part. We can ruin our own day in a matter of seconds.

Sadly, positive thoughts are more like Teflon, they tend to slide into our brain and then slip away quickly unless you know the secret to nailing them down. The secret is that you linger just a little bit longer on the blessings in your life, or what country singer Kenny Chesney called "the good stuff."²⁷

Ever wonder why there are so many Scriptures that urge us to be proactive and protective about our thoughts? The book of Proverbs urges us to guard what comes into our hearts, because out of our heart (or mind garden) flow the rivers of everything we do (4:23). God must have known that if we just "let what happens, happen" in our brains, our default mode will almost always be negative. But we can catch and keep "joy on the wing" by lingering —just a second or two longer—on the things that lift our spirits. Think of how coffee lovers pause to enjoy the ritual of making the coffee, then smell and sip the brew, perhaps saying aloud, "Ahhhh … that's good." In the same way we can take an extra pause when we hear the laughter of children or note the kindness in our husband's eyes or read an inspiring line in a book and say, "Ahhh, now that's good. Thank You, God."

Over months and years this small habit of mentally planting and watering blessings will yield a garden of gratitude. My father is one of the kindest, wisest, happiest, most balanced, and Christlike men I know. Perhaps it is not surprising that Daddy is also one of those rare men prone to pause and savor a good moment, whether it is listening to rain on the roof, delighting in my mother's ageless charm, getting misty over a line from a song, or hugging his child or grandchild just a few seconds longer than most. He has lived his life in small moments of perpetual gratitude, strung like pearls, one after another. The result is a well-nourished mind that gives joy and grace to an oft malnourished world. (We tease my dad because he savors every single bite of food and thus is not only the world's most satisfied diner, but its slowest eater.)

Another practical way to plant seeds of goodness is to create a Journal of Nourishing Thoughts and fill it with moments, memories, words, people, actions, quotes, scenes, a poem, a verse—anything you find positive and inspirational. When I'm going through a trying time, I've found it helpful to write down any "painful thoughts" that are automatically going around in my head. Then I pray and ask God to give me His "replacement thought"—a better, truer story that heals, soothes, and lifts me up. I sometimes cross out the old thought with a pen and circle the nourishing thought, just to emphasize the process of weeding out what is not helpful and planting what is. Keep your Nourishing Thoughts Journal handy and skim it often, until beautiful, wise thoughts stick to your brain and change your heart and outlook.

Act As If

I remember clearly when as a young adult I first realized that people can go through the same life experience with dread and fear, or with excitement and joy, and often the only difference was a shift in perspective or a shift in thoughts.

I used to be a mess of nerves when I thought about flying; so for many years I avoided air travel. Then one day, years ago (before there was such a thing as 9/11 or the TSA), I was at the airport standing at the big windows and watching the planes take off, glad that I was not among the passengers. A woman standing near me was looking at the same scene only she was smiling, her eyes wide with excitement. "Oh!" she said. "I'm so jealous of the people on those planes! Wouldn't you just love to be jetting away, flying about the clouds, landing somewhere new and exciting!" I must have looked at her as though she'd just sprouted a daisy from each ear. But something clicked. The next time I had to board a plane, I decided to "act as if" I were that woman, giddy with the thought of soaring away to new adventures. Before long, I found I loved to fly, and it wasn't long before I was the person offering comfort to a nervous seatmate.

Cary Grant was terribly shy, but he adopted this method of

"acting as if" and pretended he was a movie star, elegant and suave, self-assured, funny, and at ease. Apparently, it worked out well. If someone has wronged you unjustly, perhaps you could imagine yourself as Nelson Mandela. If you are getting too serious about life and need to lighten up, imagine you are Tina Fey or Dave Barry. Want to cultivate an air of mystery, style, or grace? Put on some Jackie O glasses and go for it. This mental exercise can really be fun as you think of a character with traits you admire and imagine how they'd handle a certain situation. (Of course, the most used example of this technique is "What would Jesus do?")

Worry is the waste of a good imagination. So let your creative thoughts work for you instead of against you. A helpful, fun question to ask that always gets the imagination rolling in a positive direction is, *If you woke up tomorrow and found you were suddenly living a beautifully nourished life, what would you be doing?*

Then keep asking yourself more detailed questions such as, *If you were living a deeply nourished life, how would you treat yourself and others? What would you be thinking about? What sounds would you hear? What would you smell in the air? What would your surroundings look like? What would you eat? What would be on your day planner?* This is a delightful way to daydream and figure out what may need tweaking in order for you to design a more nourished life.

RACHEL

Though Mom is going through a deep kind of sorrow right now, I'm actually mostly in a season of blessing and joy. Yesterday she said, "I am so glad you aren't going through tough stuff right now, because we need one of the two of us to remember that not everybody reading this book is in crisis. Since we're in one, and our ministry at church is to help couples in crisis, you start to think maybe the whole world is in major trouble and pain."

"No worries," I told her. "I'm thrilled to be the shallow, happy part of our writing team."

Even though my life is in a good place, my thoughts, if I let them, can take me to a bad place.

Tomorrow's Worries

Peace and joy, come what may. It sounds lovely doesn't it? Though I am enjoying a break from major loss or crisis, trust me, I've had my share of them both. For an average thirty-year-old, I've had a lot of difficult moments. I've been to funerals for five close friends under the age of twenty-five and mourned at least a handful of other young deaths that affected my community—acquaintances, brothers and sisters of classmates, classmates of my brothers. I have a more heightened awareness, based on multiple losses at a young age, that life is fragile and old age is not a guarantee. I somehow managed to emerge from all those early losses and come out on the other side with a life (and a mind) that is still mostly full of peace and joy. Still, worry and fear are my toughest innermost spiritual battles, where "brain kudzu" is most likely to start growing like wildfire ... if I let it.

Exactly one month before our wedding, Jared fell off a ladder and suffered a serious brain injury. By the end of that first day, the doctors couldn't give us any guarantees. That night, on the floor of the ICU waiting room, I thrashed around with God, pleaded, got angry. "Are You kidding me, God?" It wasn't pretty.

Eventually the waves of anger and angst passed, and I was left with the only thing I really could do. In the dark waiting room with restless visitors sleeping all around me, I opened up my palms, tears streaming down my cheeks, and whispered, "Jared is Yours, God. Your sovereign hands are more capable than mine." I was facing my worst nightmare. But in that moment I found that whatever the outcome—whether Jared died, suffered memory

loss, or underwent personality changes — God's love was sufficient to carry me through. After a scary week, Jared was cleared to
go home, and in time his brain healed completely and the wedding
went on as planned.

After that experience, I came to a place of relative peace and
wasn't as terrified of losing someone I love at any moment.

Then I became a momma ... and my old fears came back with
a vengeance. That fist I'd opened in the waiting room, that night
I gave Jared to God, closed tight like an iron lock around my
family. Things were different now. I had a child, dependent on
me in every way, whom I loved more than I dreamed I could love.
This powerful tiger-mama love changed everything. Including my
peace of mind in an unsettling way.

I wonder sometimes, *Come what may, even if a mother's worst
nightmare came to pass— would God alone be sufficient?* And then I
sense Him whispering back, "You have today, dear daughter. You
have today. Tomorrow is mine, and I don't give you grace ahead
of time for the future." Grace and strength to get through a crisis
are like manna: they come from heaven and only in big enough
quantities to last for one day.

The whole last half of the sixth chapter of Matthew is nourishment for minds that struggle with anxiety. Jesus uses colorful
word pictures that resonate with me: Jesus pointed to a field of
lilies, and using exaggeration and trademark humor, He pointed
out to His audience that He did not see these flowers huffing and
puffing, working day and night to be perfect lilies. Jesus also uses
the metaphor of birds in the air who have nary a clue how to plow
or plant seeds. They just do bird-brained things, like fly and trust
the Father will help them find food when they are hungry. He
asks if, by worrying, we can add one extra second to our lives? Or
grow an inch taller? What? Noooo?

I love the way *The Message* translates the way Jesus concludes
His most famous antianxiety sermonette:

If God gives such attention to the appearance of wildflowers
—most of which are never even seen—don't you think he'll
attend to you, take pride in you, do his best for you? What I'm
trying to do here is to get you to relax, to not be so preoccu-
pied with *getting,* so you can respond to God's *giving.* People
who don't know God and the way he works fuss over these
things, but you know both God and how he works. Steep your
life in God-reality, God-initiative, God-provisions. Don't
worry about missing out. You'll find all your everyday human
concerns will be met. Give your entire attention to what
God is doing right now, and don't get worked up about what
may or may not happen tomorrow. God will help you deal
with whatever hard things come up when the time comes.
(Matthew 6:30–34, *The Message*; emphasis in original)

Apparently, human brains only have the capacity to worry
about twelve hours of stuff at a time. I honestly can't fathom that
I'd be okay if I lost someone I loved. I can't even go there. I've
realized that doesn't mean I don't have faith in God. It just means
God doesn't want me to contemplate that today, because it is not
on today's Approved Worry List.

Worrying about worst-case scenarios is like playing the
What-If game with your husband, "Would you still love me if I
had warts all over my face?" "Would you still love me if I stopped
taking a bath?" Somebody is bound to feel like their love would
be inadequate. Thankfully, God doesn't play those silly games
with us.

If today is a bad day, we can be in it and feel it, but only the
part of it that is happening now, not the part of it that might happen or could happen tomorrow—which tends to be where all the
major weeds come from in my brain garden.

Because I like to know the rules and follow them, I like to
know that if I want to, I can fret over Today's Approved List. We
aren't weaker for it, less Christian for it. Last week, for exam-

ple, Jackson's grandma picked him up after school on an icy day. I called and texted but got no word back. I was a legitimately concerned Mama Bear, and I unashamedly sent Papa Bear to go check on Baby Bear. Who, by the way, was just fine.

So treat your mind as the treasure it is: weed it, plant it, nourish it with all good things, and "joy anyway" will follow you all the days of your life.

Chapter 14

Seasons
of Drought

Nourishing
the Brain in Pain

*In the midst of winter, I found
there was within me an invincible summer.*
Albert Camus

BECKY

Because Greg and I are in an informal ministry of companioning people through pain, we get lots of emails, texts, and phone calls from hurting souls as part of our normal routine. In the past few weeks, we've ministered to three couples who are going through major crises. They are in shock and pain, and two are now separated. Their children are in transition and hurting too. A dear friend of mine got a cancer diagnosis that sent us all reeling. Another longtime family friend, gorgeous and full of life, a mother of two, died suddenly, and completely unexpectedly, of a brain aneurysm. Yet another friend is in financial crisis since she lost her job last year, and she wrote an SOS that she was about to be evicted from her home. A precious friend, a young woman, and her one-year-old baby moved in with us this week, in need of a soft place to land as she traverses a crisis and gets back on her feet. She will likely live here for many months.

And that was just the last few weeks. I know our "normal week" is not most people's "normal week," but we would not change our life for anything in the world. We love showing up when others back away. We love nourishing people in the valley, on their way to the Land of Beginning Again. It's our calling.

And so, if you happen to be in real crisis or pain, this "sequel" chapter is for you. If you aren't currently going through drama, chances are someone you love is in a hard place. Perhaps this chapter might help you to help them, or maybe you can share it with them as a comforting gift, along with a casserole.

The blessing of a well-stored mind is that regular soul nourishment can give you wisdom and strength to hold you through difficult times. When you savor your blessings and give thanks for them during happier, easier times, you've created a mental garden of gratitude and good memories that may hold you steady during times of drought, when it can be hard to think at all.

Here are some thoughts that I've experienced to be a great comfort, that nourish a brain in a season of pain.

Nourish a Higher, Eternal Perspective

Interestingly, when my problems here on earth get me down, I find myself drawn to stories about after-death experiences. (My favorite of these is the audio version of *To Heaven and Back* by a physician, Dr. Mary C. Neal.[28]) Images of heaven soothe my frazzled nerves by reminding me that this earthly "vale of tears" is temporary; that someday all things will be made new; that I am an eternal spiritual being, having a temporary earthly experience. Imagining what matters most in heaven is like mentally boarding a hot air balloon—up, up, and away!—enabling me to get fresh perspective from a God's-eye view on what's unfolding in front of me, down on Planet Earth. After reading about how things function in heaven—ruled by God's love—I close the pages and pray, "Thy kingdom come, thy will be done, on earth as it is in heaven" (Matthew 6:10 RSV). This did not change the circumstances, but it certainly began to change me.

Bless his heart, Greg confessed one day to feeling a little nervous about my newfound fascination with heaven, worried that I might be contemplating an early exit; but I reassured him it was a clearer vision of heaven that gave me much-needed perspective in the here and now. Sometimes a long view of what really matters in eternity is the quickest way to get clarity on how to handle our problems today.

Increase Understanding and Compassion for Your Brain in Pain

Depression was a concept mostly foreign to me, as I am thoroughly sanguine by nature, your textbook Pollyanna. But over the past few months, there were weeks when I dreaded the sunrise, longing to stay wrapped in the cocoon of my soft, safe bed. Even after I'd make the gargantuan effort of getting up and dressed, I kept glancing at the clock, longing for bedtime and the blessed unconsciousness that comes with sleep. My creativity vanished, and with my brain in a fog, writing became a convoluted and impossible task. And the sleepiness! Who knew grieving could be so exhausting? I could barely fit my life into my newly jam-packed sleeping schedule.

I was so thankful for the understanding I'd gathered over the years about how painful events affect the brain. After writing two books with Dr. Earl Henslin (*This Is Your Brain on Joy* and *This Is Your Brain in Love*) and assisting the world-renown brain pioneer, Dr. Daniel Amen, in research and writing, I could actually visualize what my brain scan and Greg's probably looked like under duress.

Trauma messes with your brain chemistry and stalls connections for a season. This is why sadness can exhaust people. Newly pregnant women are amazed at how fatigued they are as their body channels its limited energy toward creating new life. In some ways, your brain is doing something similar; it is busy letting go of one "normal" and finding ways to assimilate a new "normal." It's physically tiring brain work.

As the commercial says, "Where does depression hurt? Everywhere." As hokey as that may sound, it's true. Depression affects the same areas of our brain that process physical pain. I felt it in my gut, as if I'd swallowed a giant pretzel made of rock. Emotional pain gripped Greg's chest in such a viselike squeeze a couple of times that we worried he might be having a heart attack. (You may want to see a compassionate physician to prescribe something to help ease the painful "grief spasms" and body tightness, especially through the roughest few months.)

Not only does a highly stressful or agonizing experience make you tired or achy, but it can also make you feel profoundly stupid. Neurons and dendrites and synapses and such — once available to make lists, think creatively, or focus on tasks — are now being "borrowed" for the SOS brain task of coping with a loss, processing painful emotions, and rewiring your brain to accept and adjust to new realities. While this is happening, you have precious little brain energy left over for regular tasks and social interactions. Your to-do list may shrink to getting one or two things done per day. You may lose your appetite for many things you loved: good food, reading (your brain can't absorb many words), going out. Do not despair. This is temporary. It will all come back once your brain has adjusted to the new normal. In the meantime, keep reading. Ideas for more relief follow.

Seek Out and Embrace
a More Nourishing Story

One way the brain processes upset is through telling itself stories from different angles until it settles on a narrative that fits and helps you move forward. One way you can help yourself heal is to examine the stories you tell yourself. If these looping stories are bringing up more anger, resentment, worry, or sorrow—you might want to search for some better stories. If you cling to stories that flood your body with toxic emotions, they can take you on a one-way trip to despair and bitterness. Often it is not the actual event or person that keeps on hurting us, but our "thoughts about" the event or person instead. They may have hurt us once, but by rumination, we reinjure ourselves again and again.

Jesus spent much of His ministry undoing false stories and replacing them with truer, better ones. The Sermon on the Mount is a great case in point, where He begins each thought with "You have heard that it was said,... but I tell you ..." He is, in essence, introducing fresh twists on old familiar ways of looking at life. When we exchange false, painful stories for God's truer, better ones—over time we also change our emotions, our moods, our personalities, and the outcome of our very lives.

We all know people who have experienced the exact same kind of loss or hurt, but they let it shape them in two very different ways. Same injury, but the crucial difference is one told himself a "grievance story," while the other chose a "nourishing story" about the identical event.

A fabulous example of this is my friend Shawn. She found the love of her life in midlife. But she and her Ron were married just five years before he died of complications in surgery. She was devastated and grieved his loss profoundly. Within a couple of years, however, she met another widower whose name was also Ron. Happiness returned. They married, and she moved to his country home in Alabama. He provided Shawn with her own version of

Eden, a patch of pretty tree-covered land, a garden, a cozy house with a wide front porch, and dogs. Lots of dogs. Two of her adult children soon moved nearby as well, which delighted her heart. Shawn and her children found solace and fresh hope in the happy, healing surroundings that Ron #2 provided.

Then just a few years later, this new Ron was diagnosed with pancreatic cancer and died within a few weeks.

Two husbands, both named Ron, both gone in the span of two five-year-long marriages. Shawn would be the perfect candidate for nursing her wounds, growing bitter at God, giving up on life and love and hope. One day, however, she wrote me the following email, and I knew my brave friend would find a way to rise above even this sorrow.

As I look back, I see a row of soil just like in my garden. All kinds of seeds are being dropped into the groove of earth, some good, some bad. Right behind them are these big, manly, powerful hands gently covering each seed with rich, warm, healthy soil and patting it down to perfection. That's what God does. He doesn't stop the bad stuff from happening, but He covers it up with good things and then most likely waters it with His own tears.

Losing my first husband Ron was a horrible thing. God covered it with Ron's invitation to join him in Alabama and become his wife. My adult daughter moved nearby, and her life has been changed forever, her marriage on track, her health restored. My lastborn Evan was taken from a scattered life with no future, to live near us and find a career and start a family. Jack-Henry, Evan's new son, was created from the entire situation. Only a good and loving God could accomplish those things.

Now I feel like I'm observing another "bad seed" being planted; and only God knows what good things He is conjuring to cover it up with.

Shawn could have so easily told herself stories about God's unfairness and grown sad, ugly, and bitter. Instead she prayed and asked Him for a better, truer story. And indeed, God gave her a nourishing word picture of healing and hope.

Cry Productive Tears

Did you know that tears from sadness contain actual toxins that tears of joy do not? If you feel a lump in your throat, try to let the tears flow freely as soon as you can. This is because after we've let those tears flow, those nasty toxins leave our body and a lightness returns to the body and mind—like the cool, clean air following rain. (This is why you can feel limp but also peaceful and relieved after a good hard cry.)

Remind yourself that your tears are precious to God. The psalmist tells us that God saves our tears in a bottle. The original word for this bottle is actually a "wine-making flask." God sees every teardrop, saves them like the finest grapes, then transforms your heartbroken tears into something beautiful, rich, and life-giving that will quench another's thirst and bring comfort and joy to many.

Let Go of Controlling Anything or Anyone — Except for Your Thoughts

When life hits us upside the head with a shocking bit of news, a hurt, disappointment, loss, or betrayal, most of us react with some amount of venting, some acting out or self-pity as we try to get ourselves upright again.

But at some point, we wake up to a fresh realization that we cannot control life, other people, or most circumstances. We are not in charge of much at all, really, in this world. As I said at the beginning of this chapter, however, God allows us control *over just one area of our lives*, and that is ... we get to choose our thoughts about what happens to us and how we will respond. We get this privilege almost every second of every day of our lives. It is no small gift. We can cocreate with God new ways to process what happens to us, totally changing our experience of it.

It has been said that there are two kinds of pain: clean pain and dirty pain. Clean pain is acknowledging a painful event that legitimately hurts. But once we've vented to someone safe and cried our lot of tears, we move forward to the nourishing work of letting go, forgiving, visualizing new dreams and better ways of being, trusting God to repurpose our pain into something even more beautiful. Dirty pain is when we create ongoing "grievance stories" about what happened to us, then go over it in our minds, nursing grudges, staying stuck, and therefore, continuing to reinjure ourselves with our painful thoughts long after the event transpired.

Rock Your Soul

More and more scientists are understanding that a trauma doesn't just lodge in the brain alone, it permeates cells all over our body. This is why we may be triggered by an event (or smell or sound) that links to an old painful memory, never consciously processing it in our brain. It has become a body memory. My most traumatic memories from my time in Texas include country songs playing in the background. (Country music, like pickup trucks, permeates the Lone Star State.) At the time I didn't make any conscious connection between painful experiences and the music that played in the background.

Interestingly, however, many years later, just a few strains of any country song on the radio can make me feel sad, agitated, and anxious all at once. Greg has learned that if he doesn't want to mess with my happy mood on car trips, it's best to avoid turning the dial anywhere near a country music station.

I bet you've discovered something similar: a smell or a song, a scene in a movie, or a tone in someone's voice can trigger feelings from long-ago pain in the very cells of your body. Perhaps your stomach tenses up or your eyes water or your mood drops. And it may take your brain a few minutes to comprehend what's happening on a logical level. This is what body memories are like. The "trauma" could even be fairly benign. My husband feels nauseous at the sight of green beans. He worked summers in a green-bean cannery and got his fill of green beans for a lifetime.

A variety of trauma specialists from all parts of the world have found that one simple way to help people to release trauma, especially when it is held in the body, is to do some form of back-and-forth swaying movement. Scientists aren't completely sure why this works; they only know that it does. I think it all stems back to the way we were soothed as babies when we were swaddled and rocked or bounced or put in a swing. I sometimes wonder if Jesus, the Master Teacher and Healer, spent lots of time in boats and walking with His disciples because the waves of the water and the rhythm of walking allowed their minds to relax as He shared stories of heaven's truth with them and asked them questions to ponder.

Engaging the large muscles also releases neurotransmitters that calm stress: doing pull-ups or calf raises (up on toes, then flat on feet, repeat) and even carrying something heavy—like books in a backpack—can send relaxing messages to an amped-up brain. One researcher and author of the book *Lifting Depression* discovered that doing something productive and repetitive with your hands—knitting, stirring, vacuuming, shelling peas, quilting—engages something she calls the Effort Driven Reward Loop and is calming and mood lifting.[29]

A practical way to use this information is to notice when you are caught in a negative or painful thought loop. Then go for a walk, do a few push-ups, get out your knitting, vacuum the carpet, or mow the lawn. Or you can even do simple breathing with your belly, in and out. I've always found calm around the rhythm of water, whether it is doing the backstroke as I float in a pool or watching ocean waves roll and swoosh. Even watching fish swimming rhythmically, back and forth, in a fish tank can calm the brain.

Don't tell anyone (this will be our little secret), but when I get overwhelmed by painful looping thoughts that don't seem to stop in the middle of the night, I'll go to another room in the house and swing my arms back and forth like a gorilla, or side to side like a rag doll, until I feel calm enough to go back to bed. Works like a charm. Thus far, Greg's never caught me in my monkey act. (Don't knock it until you've tried it!)

Latch on to whatever repetitive movement you enjoy that soothes your brain. Once you are in a more neutral and calm state, it is the perfect time to spend a few moments in prayer or to listen to a comforting piece of music or to get out your Nourishing Thoughts Journal and read through it. You've calmed your brain with movement, and now you are much more receptive to better stories, positive truth, healing words. You may also find this is a good time to try out the next couple of points and exercises.

Find Visual Metaphors That Calm You

The mind actually thinks in pictures, so when you can visualize a story or a word picture, the brain can latch on to an abstract concept much easier. I love the image of Jesus asleep in the boat in the midst of a terrific storm. He had not one worry, just snoozing away. And then when He woke up and saw the commotion, He calmingly said, "Peace, be still." Waves, thunder, and the fast-beating hearts of the frightened men ... became instantly calm. When I am afraid, my mind can lock in on the scene of Jesus sleeping in the boat, and I sometimes imagine that I'm tucked in His arms, where there is no fear, no matter how the storm rages.

I believe the Twenty-Third Psalm is so beloved by people in grief or pain because of the rich word pictures it creates: a kind and comforting shepherd leading his beloved lamb through the dark valley, making sure this hurting lamb gets to rest in green valleys and her thirst is quenched by a pool of blue water. For those who have felt the sting of betrayal, the picture of Jesus Himself preparing a table and a feast just for you, "in the presence of your enemies," is one that reminds you that God sees you and values you and honors you no matter what others around you may think.

On another day when I was feeling completely overwhelmed, I got a visual picture that has been a comfort to me for many months. Perhaps it might also comfort and nourish you. I imagined all the things I need to do, and people I care about, as an array of multicolored bowls on a lazy Susan in the middle of a round table. Then I see myself sitting at the table where God turns the lazy Susan: my job, then, is to focus only on the bowl He's put in front of me that day. The other bowls — the ones currently out of reach — are being tended to by others (on the other sides of God's big table) and are not part of my particular "job" or "focus" for this day.

Each day, God gives us our daily bowl. Tomorrow we wake to a new bowl. To reach beyond that, across the table, to bowls that aren't meant to be in our frame of concerns, tends to make a big mess.

Keep an eye out for images and word pictures that soothe you — from sermons, novels, or a scene in a movie — and jot them (or sketch them) in your journal. Or ask God to give you a comforting mental picture, as He gave to my friend Shawn who lost her beloved Rons.

RACHEL

Nourish Your Mind with Acts of Self-Care

When you go through the tough times, your thoughts can get so kidnapped and overfocused on the crisis at hand that you forget to do even the little things that nourish your mind with tender loving acts of self-care. Just as my mom has done for me during difficult seasons, this time around I've encouraged her to tend to herself, to put the writing of this book, other people's crises, and even the world on hold, until she has taken care of herself.

It's a good idea, in fact, for everyone to create a list of Ten Things to Soothe Your Soul.

Here is a list of ideas to get you started. You may want to draw some ideas from this list, but it is helpful for everyone to create their own unique, favorite list of calming activities. Keep it somewhere so you can see it and visit it regularly.

- Sit outside in the sun, watch the clouds roll by.
- Take a hot bubble bath with vanilla or lavender scent.
- Organize one thing: your purse, a drawer, your jewelry.
- Go for a walk, a bike ride, or a drive in the country.
- Meet a friend who is a good listener.
- Get a massage.
- Play in a sandbox.
- Cuddle or walk a pet.
- Talk to a counselor, wise mentor, spiritual director, trusted pastor, or life coach.
- Read books that lift your spirits. My mom loves travel memoirs that take her away to the streets of Paris or hillsides of Tuscany. She also loves books about happiness, resilience, joy, and thriving. Give me some healthy cookbooks or some mom humor or a writer who is vulnerable about life and faith. Read what leaves you feeling better.
- Quilt, knit, crochet.
- Read a funny book or watch a comedy show.
- Play a musical instrument.
- Take a class in something that interests you: painting, pottery, learning Italian!

- Buy or pick flowers and arrange them.
- Browse through Pinterest, watch Food Network shows, try new recipes. (Can we boldly recommend our funny mother-daughter food memoir, *We Laugh, We Cry, We Cook*?[30])
- Babysit for someone if babies or children lift your spirits — the offer would most certainly lift the spirits of many young moms I know.
- Take a guilt-free nap — if it is a pretty day, buy yourself a hammock and enjoy a nature nap. If it is cold outside, treat yourself to a soft, heated throw or blanket and relax into dreamland.
- Take a training class that will help you to heal and also minister to others (Stephen Ministries is one such source, but there are many).
- Attend a recovery group. My church highly recommends that all members go through their Steps Program, not just addicts. We all have something in our past that we need to recover from, make peace with, repent of, forgive. In fact, they would say that if you think you don't need a recovery group, you may be the one who needs it most.
- Try centering, calming prayer. During a high-anxiety time in my life, my mom gave me two CDs by Nigel Mumford, who is an Episcopal priest with a heart to help God's children find emotional healing. One is called "Relaxation and Healing Prayer" and the other is "The Essence of Soaking Prayer." Nigel's comforting British accent reads Scriptures and prayers as soft music plays. (See http:// byhiswoundsministry.org/.)

Never underestimate the value of "healthy diversions" when you are in a crisis or recovering from one. These seemingly small but comforting activities allow your tired or wounded mind to take a break from painful thoughts or automatic ruminating. Most of all, remember that recovering from loss or sadness, especially of the traumatic variety, takes time, patience, rest, gentleness, and pampering. An overwhelmed or hurting mind deserves the same consideration we give to those who have been physically injured or have been through a rough surgery. If ever there is a time to slow down and focus on what nourishes you most—it is in seasons of recovery.

Eventually, the garden of your mind will heal and blossom again.

Chapter 15

He Calls
Me Darlin'

The Nourishing Voice
of God

And so we know and rely on
the love God has for us. God is love.
Whoever lives in love lives in God,
and God in them.

1 John 4:16

RACHEL

Between Jared's large family and mine, Jackson is surrounded by lots of love. When I tallied up the number of close family coming to his first birthday party, the list pushed forty people, including all seven of his living great-grandparents. I worried he'd be overwhelmed with so many people. I planned to take him to the nursery for a little break in case the "madding crowd" proved too much for him.

Boy, was I wrong.

The kid knew how to be celebrated, how to be delighted in, how to accept hugs and high fives and presents. Oh, how he loved opening his presents, peeling the paper back slowly to draw out the fun, followed by a little happy dance of gratitude. His eyes darted from one person to the next, not in a "Who are these people?" kind of way, but in a "Who's the lucky guest who gets to play with me next?" kind of way. I kept losing track of him as he moved with ease from one adoring family member to the next.

Thus surrounded by fans, it would never cross his mind that people would not be delighted to get to meet him or spend time with him. He waves to everyone as we walk down grocery aisles or airport terminals. He shows great concern for the health of people who don't respond back. "He can't wave, Mama." Translation: "Quite obviously that person's arm is not functioning, because surely if he *could* wave, he would."

My child is so at ease in the world right now because he's never known anything but clans of adoring relatives. However, we were together at the park the other day, and I felt a pang in my heart when I witnessed a little boy, a couple years older than Jackson, being mean to him. Jackson was mimicking the boy, swinging from the bars and climbing up the slide like him, making the same "big-boy-in-action" noises. Of course, in Jackson's world, imitation is the sincerest form of flattery, but apparently the other child didn't get that memo.

When I heard the boy tell Jackson, "You're annoying," I wanted to rush in like a mother eagle and swoop my baby up to the top of the jungle … uh … gym.

Jackson, in his innocence, handled the situation expertly. "Annoying?" he asked, trying on the sound of the syllables. "What is *annoying*?"

The kid responded, "Um, it means, um, um, well I don't really know what it means, okayyyyy?" That silenced the little vocabulary whiz, but I know there will be other bullies, and it won't be long before he understands the insults or realizes someone's arm isn't broken when they don't wave at him.

My mother assured me that even though he'll go out into the

world and kids will sometimes be mean to him, the foundation of love and belonging will hold him steady. Jared and I will help him process the truth that hurting people hurt people, and show him how to recover from the "slings and arrows" of Mean Kids.

We will continue to remind him that he is delightful, that he brightens our world simply by being in it, that no mean kid or gossip or bad choice will change our minds on that issue. He is ours.

In her poignant, hilarious book about the first year of being a mother, Anne Lamott wrote, "I don't remember who said this, but there really are places in the heart you don't even know exist until you love a child."[31]

I've also realized that there are depths of God's love and His nourishing nature that you can't understand until you deeply love a child or long for a child to love.

BECKY

God's Favorites

I laughed at a bumper sticker I once saw. It was bright yellow, had a smiley face on it, and cheerily declared, "God loves you!" But in parenthesis, there was an additional line, in smaller print: "But He loves me most." At first glance, I thought, *How funny, but how narcissistic.* But upon further mulling, I wonder if that might not be exactly the way God wants us to feel.

Stay with me; I am going somewhere with this.

I recently came to realize, with some measure of gladness and satisfaction, that each of my grown children had assumed they were my "favorite child"—which is exactly as it should be. It let me know that I had done at least a few things right as a mother. And they are absolutely correct: each and every one of them is my favorite child.

In the book *The Shack*, the God "figure" is played by an African

American woman, and she has an endearing way of talking about each of her "children" and adding, "I'm especially fond of that one." The main character, Mack, begins to notice this trend and asks her at one point, "Are there any you are not especially fond of?"

She answers, "Nope, I haven't been able to find any. Guess that's jes' the way I is."[32]

Could it be that God is "especially fond" of each of us and that we are, every one individually, his most favorite child?

I find it interesting that the apostle John referred to himself, over five times, as "the disciple Jesus loved" or "the beloved disciple." His identity, his name, after so many years with Christ, was simply, "The one Jesus loves." I cannot help but wonder if the other disciples might each have believed they were Christ's favorite too, that he was "especially fond" of them as well. Or perhaps John was so focused on the great love of God, he wanted to make a point by replacing his own name with a description of his belongingness. When you abide, which means to "settle down to make yourself at home" in God's love, your whole identity changes. Your central role in life is no longer Becky or Rachel or "mom" or "wife" or "writer," but the older you get and more you allow God's love to seep in to your very pores, the more your identity becomes "the beloved daughter of God."

Try tacking on this "beloved" identity to your own name, just for fun. Here, I'll go first. "Hello, I am Becky, the Woman Jesus Loves. But for short, some people just called me Becky the Beloved." Now you try it, with your name. Feels pretty awesome, doesn't it?

Three Things Every Child (of God) Needs to Hear

The Scriptures record only one time that God spoke aloud from heaven to Jesus where others could also hear Him. He said only one sentence, but in that sentence is everything a child longs to hear from his parent: "You are my Son, whom I love; with you I am well pleased" (Mark 1:11). In these few words, the heavenly Father blessed His son in three vital ways:

1. He publically gave Christ an identity and seal of belonging. "You are *my* son."
2. He deeply loved His son.
3. He took great delight in His son, and was thoroughly pleased with Him.

Child psychiatrists will tell you that the things children need most to grow up emotionally healthy are to know they belong to a family, to know they are cherished and loved, and even more than loved—that they are thoroughly liked. That their presence brings joy to their parent's face. One translation of the most famous of Hebrew blessings says, "May the Lord bless and protect you; may the Lord's *face radiate with joy because of you*" (Numbers 6:25 TLB, emphasis added).

I came upon a picture of Rachel recently and couldn't stop admiring it. Jackson was about three months old. Rachel was sitting on a porch in the morning sun. Jackson had that milk-blissed look of pure adoration in his eyes as he gazed at his mother, the giver of all things tasty and nourishing. And she returned his gaze with equal delight. She had an assuring smile that said to her son, "You are my one and only boy. I love you to the moon and back. And just being with you tickles me to death." Rachel's face literally radiated with joy because of her child.

Can you imagine that photo? Now, for just a minute, try to imagine God's face in place of Rachel's and you as the child. Can you see God's face "radiating with joy because of you"—just because you are His, and your very being brings Him pure delight? Because if you can, you will begin to see the healing, nourishing side of God.

Terms of Endearment

I've been blessed with an earthly father who is one of those rare men who loves people deeply and has no problem expressing it. My mother too is equally loving. What this means is that I grew up bookended by two parents who cherished me, told me they loved me every day, and showed their love in a million tangible ways over the years. Because I was loved well, and my parents also loved each other deeply and openly, I grew up to be a person who is "porous" for love. When people said they loved me, I had no reason to doubt the truth of it, so I took it in. My foundational identity was, "I am George and Ruthie's beloved daughter. They proudly claim me as their child, they love me dearly, and they get a big kick out of being around me. They've always told me the truth, and they taught me God loves me, so I also believe this to be true."

My dad often calls or writes or refers to me as "Becky Darlin'," and over the years I've absorbed this as my deepest identity. Greg also calls me "Darlin'," and every time he does, it echoes back to my father's love and then to my heavenly Father's love, and another little part of me heals. In my mind, in my prayers, God too calls me "Darlin'," and I call Him Kind Father. And as I remember that, deep places in my heart find healing.

All of us have endured traumas, big and small, and each one affects our brain chemistry at some level. To be bereft of comfort or love after trauma, however, sears our brains with pain; the way we view our world can become skewed and harsh and fearful. But God's heart is to never leave us comfortless, and we can heal when we are truly seen, heard, allowed our voice, and treated with respect by someone willing to be a warm vessel for God's love.

In other words, we heal as we see ourselves "precious in His sight." Then, in time, we become Wounded Healers to others. We can stand in the gap for El Roi, "The God Who Sees Me" ... as we look deeper at one another and point out the beauty we find there.

One evening I convinced Greg to watch one of my all-time favorite films with me, *Enchanted April*. The movie is about four women in the 1920s who, each longing for an escape from their lives, pool their money together to rent an Italian villa by the sea, "San Salvatore." (I realized that even the name of the villa, "Savior," foreshadowed what was to come.)

Lottie, the discontented but lovable wife—who was the most anxious to flee her life for a month—is the first to wake to lost joy as she allows the beauty of sea, flowers, and hills to melt and soften her heart. Then, as she soaks in this balm and feels herself wholly beloved, she meanders in and out of the other characters' lives. She says to each person, in her own way—no matter how cranky or disconnected, vain or insensitive they are (in the midst of their brokenness and ugliness)—"I see inside you, I see the real you. And you are unbelievably precious. In time, you'll see it too. I just know it." She becomes a sort of Christ-figure in the movie, touching every character and leaving them with a feeling of having been truly seen, messiness and all, and found worthy of love and tenderness. In time, loved by a human friend and rocked in the lap of nature, each woman awakens to love and beauty, and one by one, each experiences their own unique April of the soul.

At the end of the movie a formerly bitter old lady, now feeling youthfully alive, leaves behind her walking stick, jamming it into the dirt. We see, through high speed film, that it blossoms into a flowering tree. An old walking cane, returned to its original purpose, to be the trunk from which flowers draw their nourishment. A symbol of how the warmth of love can repurpose our old wounds, bringing us back to Eden and the way life was originally intended to be. When one woman heals, says an old proverb, she heals seven generations. I do not know if this is true, but I know when one woman deeply realizes her belovedness as a child of God, her very presence is nourishing to others.

He's Been Waiting for You, All Your Life

On a recent tumultuous evening, I tossed and turned most of the night, my stomach in a pretzel, my mind ping-ponging, my emotions zinging, until around 4:15 when I went back to sleep, deeply.

And then I had a dream that was so real and so vivid, I woke with the lingering feeling of having been cocooned in pure love. I don't claim this as anything more than a dream, but I can tell you that God has used it to comfort and assure me in ways I will never forget.

In my dream I was flying on a cloud-like disk, and the feeling was both exhilarating and frightening. I sensed I was trying to enjoy the adventure of the ride but at the same time fighting a lingering sadness and fear and sense of being abandoned and alone.

Then a voice on a loudspeaker called my name and asked that I return to the ground. I could see, as I returned to earth, that there were a few men, dressed in black, waiting for me. I felt a sense of dread and resignation to my fate. I assumed they were there to take me to a courtroom, where I would be tried and condemned.

But to my shock, as I followed the men, I found myself in a large open space lit with a soft rosy glowing light. I suddenly realized I had no clothes, and in that very instant, a long rectangle of gorgeous silk appeared and wrapped itself around my body, like a gold-spun sari.

Once again I found myself in flight, but without any "saucer" and following the most gorgeous wide, winding, and looping street of gold at lightning speed, swooping and sailing, carefree and calm this time. In the space around me, the atmosphere was cozy and perfectly warm and lovely and I could hear voices telling me that I was loved, had always been loved, and that every tear I cried had been received with compassion, that not only God, but "they" (angels? a "cloud of witnesses"?) too saw me, *really saw me*, and that my voice was heard, and it mattered. I knew then, I was in heaven or some part or facsimile of it.

At some point the voices mentioned, "We once saw you reading a book that your father wrote."

"Yes," I said. "It is called *Between Two Worlds*."

They just smiled and nodded, as if the meaning of this conversation would be revealed and be helpful to me. Then the voices told me with excitement that God had been waiting in joyful anticipation for this moment to see me and give me everything my heart desired. And again, I felt overwhelmed knowing that I had always been seen and heard and loved and delighted in.

At the end of the golden road were stacks and stacks of treasure ... and my husband, Greg, standing beside them, smiling, the greatest of all the treasures. My heart felt it might burst with gratitude at this glorious change of events, the feeling of being wholly lavished with love instead of condemned or just barely let in the back door of heaven. I knew I was getting a glimpse of true grace, unlike anything we can imagine here. Grace and mercy in heaven does not feel at all like we go through a court trial, where we accept our portion of condemnation and judgment and sit before a replay of all our weakness and faults in living color and then are "set free" out of mercy ... barely escaping, but mindful of how much we owe God.

Instead, at least in my dream, there was the overwhelming awareness that there is truly *no* condemnation in Christ's love. At *all*. No strings are attached to our sins or any remembrance of them. We are, in fact, treated as if we are the longed for, waited for, Chosen Child. As if all our life God was excitedly waiting for this moment to shower us with goodness and love. Adopted, chosen, welcomed, and celebrated. Nothing of the past brought into the marvelous Now.

None of the riches piled up compared to the feeling of being loved without even a glimmer of judgment, loved with the same kind of open delight we feel for our children. The same sort of delight I sense in my husband's eyes, and he in mine. It was a settled calm love, but much more than just being accepted. I felt … precious. When I awoke, the dream was gone but the feelings of being rocked, soothed, cherished … lingered. It feels almost like too much love to handle, but what can you do but gaze back at the Source and soak it all in?

And so my after-dream thoughts are this: while we may "groan" in our earth suits full of hurts and flaws, and experience some crisis or tragedy or relational pain for a few more years, one day we won't "see through a cloud darkly" but we will all see God and be fully seen by Him, face to face. No more tears. No more hurt. Just pure love and delight. And maybe then, if not now, our confusing and messy earth journeys will make sense. Or maybe it just won't matter anymore. Maybe we will simply be free of all that keeps us from soaring.

One more thing: the book. As I came to consciousness, in that dreamy state between sleep and wakefulness, I thought of the conversation I had with the angelic voices about my father's book. The title, *Between Two Worlds*, and its meaning were instantly clear. The older my father (and my mother) get, the more they live with one foot on earth, one in heaven. And the secret of rising above the accumulation of our sufferings on earth as we age is living with a little less of our feet (what matters to us) planted on earth, and more and more of our feet (what matters most) inching toward heaven. So that when death comes we just scooch over the tiniest bit, to land in the rosy golden light of God's nourishing love, where at some level we've always known we truly belong.

RACHEL

My favorite video of Jackson is one I took just a few months ago. I already have it tagged as the opening scene of his video montage for his high school graduation party. In it, Jared asks Jackson what his name is. "I can't say dat word," Jackson says with a shy giggle.

"Yes, you can," I gently encourage him, sounding out his name, "Jackson. Ray. Randolph."

"Jatsonrey Ranrolf," he repeats back, then smiles wide, beaming with pride.

Tonight I tried Mom's suggestion of adding a "title" to the end of my name.

"Rachel, the One Jesus Loves." Hmmm, "Rachel the Beloved." Why does that feel so presumptuous? Like being called "Cora, Countess of Grantham." My first reaction to reading my name framed as God's object of affection is to giggle, shy away, say, "I can't say dat word." But then I remembered how much joy it brought me to hear Jackson identify himself for the very first time, saying his whole name, the one that identifies him as belonging to us, that says he is Rachel and Jared Ray Randolph's son.

And I can almost hear God urging me now. "Yes, Darlin', I know you can say it. Rachel. Randolph. The One Jesus Loves. Rachel, My Beloved Daughter. Try it again."

And so I do, and it seems to fit better each time I say it. And I'm beginning to sense my Father's smiling response: "That's my girl!"

Your Own Nourishing Path

Nourish beginnings, let us nourish beginnings....
The blessing is in the seed.

Muriel Rukeyser

RACHEL

And so we come to the end of the book, which Mom and I pray will jump-start new adventures in nourishing yourself, your surroundings, your relationships, and your soul.

Where to begin? I'd ask you, "Where do you struggle the most? What is hurting or irritating you, stealing your peace on a daily basis?"

If you cannot find your way through the maze of mess in your surroundings, or you are living in a space that does not energize you, soothe you, or reflect your personality, a home makeover (or cleanup) is an excellent place to start. Room by room, closet by closet, drawer by drawer, at whatever pace fits your life ... until you feel at home in your surroundings.

If you can't even think about making time for a home makeover because your schedule is packed fuller than a first-time mom's diaper bag, maybe a date with your day planner is in order.

Or maybe you are tripped up, around 5:00 p.m. every day, over and over with the surprise that you have to make dinner for your family … again. Nothing is thawed, you get cranky, everybody's blood sugar is low, and the family table is a zoo. In that case, start by making a menu plan for the week, write your grocery list, and get to the store. Then work on applying Mom's tips for a relaxing, tear-free table experience.

Is it your body that's bringing you down? Is your relationship with *you* suffering? Begin the important journey of self-acceptance, seeing yourself through A-plus beholders. Lovingly nourish your body through movement you enjoy and pampering that makes you feel like the woman God designed you to be.

When you have focused on nourishing *you* and made your calendar reflect your priorities, then you can begin focusing on pouring into your relationships with your husband, your children, and your friends.

Or maybe your surroundings, your schedule, your relationships are going pretty well, but what brings you down is an "under-nourished" inner life. Because even if you have the most amazing life, if your thoughts about that life bring you into negative mind loops, you may need to work on nourishing the garden of your mind.

Finally, if you struggle to believe you matter deeply, that your truest identity is as God's Beloved Child, practice saying your name with the "family title" attached, until you can say it smoothly, with a confident, happy smile. Because, of all the things we've shared in this book, we know there's nothing more beautiful, no more nourishing presence on earth, than a woman who lives loved, who knows her Father calls her Darlin' and loves to shower her with reminders of His tender caring.

God made the world for the delight of human beings—
if we could see His goodness everywhere, His concern for us,
His awareness of our needs: the phone call we've waited for,
the ride we are offered, the letter in the mail, just the little things
He does for us throughout the day. As we remember and notice
His love for us, we just begin to fall in love with Him because
He is so busy with us—you just can't resist Him. I believe there's
no such thing as luck in life; it's God's love, it's His.

Mother Teresa

Acknowledgments

We could never attempt to live nourished lives, or write a nourishing book, without a nourishing village of support.

We are enormously grateful to those who surrounded, cheered, dusted us off, hugged, encouraged, and helped us as we wholeheartedly threw ourselves into this project.

Greg Johnson: Not only are you a steady, sheltering oak-tree-of-a-husband to Becky's flitting-around butterfly-of-a-wife, you are an awesome stepdad to Rachel and a total rock star as our literary agent. (Not to forget: a fun-loving Poppy to Jackson.) We are so grateful for the many roles you play in our family and deeply appreciate the professional role you play in our writing careers.

Jared Randolph: You are the dream husband and son-in-law. You take care of Rachel and Jackson in all the important big ways and in endless "little" ways that nourish a marriage and a family. Thank you for praying for us, encouraging us, and being such an amazing hands-on dad. Many pages were written while you took Jackson with you grocery shopping—to give Rachel writing time and to replenish the necessary coffee and kale reserves—or while you played ball, or pretended to Weed Eat and mow the lawn with the most enthusiastic lawn boy around. We love you, Jared.

Carolyn McCready: What can we say? We have been spoiled by the best. Truly, you have nourished this book alongside us every step of the way. From brainstorming ideas to helping fuzzy concepts take on clarity and shape, guiding us gently away from land mines, cheering us on when we caught our stride, and editing the book in ways that made us say to each other, time and again, in some form: "Wow. That Carolyn McCready is really ... kinda ...

brilliant." You get us. We trust you. We work together like peas and carrots and corn.

Bob Hudson: Thank you for bringing your detailed eye and personal enthusiasm to this manuscript. To everyone at Zondervan, from editorial, marketing, and publicity, to cover design and more—we are grateful.

We are blessed to be surrounded by a family that loves stories, loves to laugh, and nourishes us soul and spirit. Special thank-yous to George and Ruthie (Becky's mom and dad, Rachel's grandparents) and Rachel St. John-Gilbert (Becky's sister, Rachel's namesake and aunt) and Gabriel and Aleksandria (Becky's youngest son and daughter-in-law; Rachel's little brother and sister-in-law) for extra doses of love, support, and encouragement during some incredibly tough challenges this year.

A special thanks to all those who offered their love and time with generous offers to watch Jackson during busy deadline weeks: Rhonda and Jim Randolph, Scott and Pat Freeman, Jamie Willis, and Michalla Revland. And of course, a huge thank you to Jackson's Mother's Day Out teachers, Miss Heidi and Miss Tara.

Also, thank you to the friends who have nourished our hearts through good times and rough patches during the writing of this book: Lindsey O'Connor, Michele Cushatt, Lucille Zimmerman, Ingrid Schneider, Laura Karlis, Reagan Mariani; Michelle Rusch, Melissa Gantt, and Rachel's Home Group and MOPS Mama-Friends. Also, we must say thank you to the dozens of Facebook friends who follow us—who laugh at our latest crazy status updates and comfort us with kind words on down days. You are the internet version of beloved aunties and uncles who keep us encouraged, putting fresh gas in our writing tanks each week.

A special thank you to Jackson Ray Randolph. We really should be cutting you in on a percentage of the profits because you are a daily gold mine of writing material. Instead, we promise to keep you supplied in all the toy lawn mowers and Weed Eaters your heart desires. We adore you, sweet boy!

Notes

1. Bill O'Hanlon, *Do One Thing Different* (New York: Morrow, 1999), 19.

2. John Eldredge, *The Sacred Romance* (Nashville: Nelson, 1997), 57.

3. This line is usually attributed to Anaïs Nin, but it is found nowhere in her works. According to the *Anaïs Nin Blog*, the line was actually written in 1979 by Elizabeth Appell, who was director of public relations for the John F. Kennedy University in Orinda, California, http://anaisninblog.skybluepress.com/2013/03/who-wrote-risk-is-the-mystery-solved/.

4. Anne Lamott, *Help, Thanks, Wow: The Three Essential Prayers* (New York: Riverhead, 2012), 21.

5. Peter Walsh, *Does This Clutter Make My Butt Look Fat?* (Pymble, NSW, Australia: Simon & Schuster, 2008), 20.

6. Iris Murdoch, *The Sea, the Sea* (New York: Penguin Books, 1978), 8.

7. Anne Lamott, "A Day at the Beach with My 'Aunties,'" *Salon.com*, June 5, 1997, http://www.salon.com/1997/06/05/lamott970605/.

8. Becky Johnson and Rachel Randolph, *We Laugh, We Cry, We Cook* (Grand Rapids, Mich.: Zondervan, 2013), 9–10.

9. Becky Johnson and Rachel Randolph, "Simple Lentil Soup," *welaughwecrywecook.com*, http://welaughwecrywecook.com/2013/05/09/simple-lentil-soup/.

10. Becky Johnson and Rachel Randolph, "Rustic Iron Skillet Pot Pie," *welaughwecrywecook.com*, http://welaughwecrywecook.com/2012/04/06/homestyle-iron-skillet-pot-pie/.

11. To download a pdf of this helpful Environmental Working Group "Shopper's Guide to Pesticides in Produce," also known as the Dirty Dozen list of foods to avoid, go to http://www.ewg.org/foodnews/summary.php.

12. Becky Johnson and Rachel Randolph, "Mexican Comfort Casserole and Cashew Queso," *welaughwecrywecook.com*, http://welaughwecrywecook.com/2012/04/03/mexican-comfort-casserole-cashew-queso/.

13. Pamela Druckerman, *Bringing Up Bebe: One American Mother Discovers the Wisdom of French Parenting* (New York: Penguin, 2012).

14. Michele Cushatt, *Undone: A Story of Making Peace with an Unexpected Life* (Grand Rapids, Mich.: Zondervan, 2015).

15. Lucille Zimmerman, *Renewed: Finding Your Inner Happy in an Overwhelmed World* (Nashville: Abingdon, 2013).

16. Lindsey O'Connor, *The Long Awakening: A Memoir* (Grand Rapids, Mich.: Revell, 2013).

17. Rachel Bertsche, *MWF Seeking BFF: My Yearlong Search for a New Best Friend* (New York: Ballantine Books, 2011), xii.

18. Sheila McCraith, "10 Things I Learned When I Stopped Yelling at My Kids," *The Orange Rhino Challenge*, March 12, 2013, http://theorangerhino.com/10-things-i-learned-when-i-stopped-yelling-at-my-kids/.

19. Lawrence J. Cohen, *Playful Parenting* (New York: Ballantine, 2008), 1-2.

20. Dr. Earl Henslin with Becky Johnson, *This Is Your Brain on Joy: A Revolutionary Program for Balancing Mood, Restoring Brain Health, and Nurturing Spiritual Growth* (Nashville: Nelson, 2008) and Dr. Earl Henslin with Becky Johnson, *This Is Your Brain in Love:*

New Scientific Breakthroughs for a More Passionate and Emotionally Healthy Marriage (Nashville: Nelson, 2009).

21. Shaunti Feldhahn, *For Women Only: What You Need to Know about the Inner Lives of Men, Revised and Updated Edition* (Colorado Springs: Multnomah, 2013).

22. Shaunti and Jeff Feldhahn, *For Men Only: A Straightforward Guide to the Inner Lives of Women, Revised and Updated Edition* (Colorado Springs: Multnomah, 2013).

23. Hilda Hutcherson, *What Your Mother Never Told You about S-e-x* (New York: Perigee, 2003).

24. Joseph Dillow, Linda Dillow, Lorraine Pintus, Peter Pintus, *Intimacy Ignited: Conversations Couple to Couple: Fire Up Your Sex Life with the Song of Solomon* (Colorado Springs: NavPress, 2004).

25. Winifred Gallagher, *Rapt: Attention and the Focused Life* (New York: Penguin, 2010), 3, 53.

26. Gallagher, *Rapt*, 14.

27. This concept of "Velcro" and "Teflon" came from a book called *Hardwiring Happiness* by Rick Hanson, Ph.D. (New York: Random House, 2013), 25.

28. Mary C. Neal, *To Heaven and Back: A Doctor's Extraordinary Account of Her Death, Heaven, Angels, and Life Again: A True Story* (Colorado Springs: WaterBrook, 2012).

29. Kelly Lambert, *Lifting Depression: A Neuroscientist's Hands-On Approach to Activating Your Brain's Healing Power* (New York: Basic Books, 2007).

30. Becky Johnson and Rachel Randolph, *We Laugh, We Cry, We Cook* (Grand Rapids, Mich.: Zondervan, 2013).

31. Anne Lamott, *Operating Instructions: A Journal of My Son's First Year* (New York: Ballantine, 1993), 214.

32. William P. Young, *The Shack* (Newbury Park, Calif.: Windblown Media, 2007), 119.

We Laugh, We Cry, We Cook

A Mom and Daughter Dish about the Food That Delights Them and the Love That Binds Them

Becky Johnson and Rachel Randolph

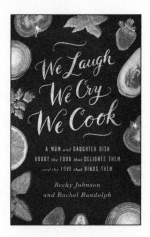

Becky Johnson and her daughter, Rachel Randolph, couldn't be more different.

Becky is messy; Rachel craves order. Becky forgets what month it is; Rachel is an organizational genius. But in the kitchen, they are in sync ... until Rachel tells her bacon-and butter-loving mama that she and her sports-jock husband have decided to go vegan. This, in a tiny Texas town where "organic" and "whole foods" are terms as unfathomable to the locals as a cool breeze in August.

In *We Laugh, We Cry, We Cook*, Becky and Rachel share stories of their fun and oft-crazy lives as Rachel becomes a mother herself. Though their differences in personality sometimes cause a clash or two, the family funny bone—plus generous helpings of grace and acceptance—keep them from taking themselves too seriously. Sprinkled throughout are delicious and nourishing recipes they love to make and share.

> "*We Laugh, We Cry, We Cook* made me want to cook, made me want to call my mom, and made me want to gather the people I love into my home and around my table with courage and honesty and hugs."
>
> —*Shauna Niequist, author of Bread & Wine*

Available in stores and online!

Contact Information

For information about this book and more see:
www.nourishedthebook.com

Becky and Rachel blog about all things nourishing—
food, laughter, and insights at:
www.welaughwecrywecook.com

Rachel has started a new blog with an
emphasis on nourishing parents-in-the-trenches at:
www.thenourishedmama.com